PERFECTING YOUR WALK IN RETIREMENT

10 STEPS TO A WORRYFREE RETIREMENT ™

by

Tony Walker

© 2006 Tony Walker. All Rights Reserved.

No part of this book may be reproduced, stored in a retrieval system, or transmitted by any means without the written permission of the author.

First published by AuthorHouse 12/28/05

ISBN: 1-4259-0889-6 (e)
ISBN: 1-4259-0888-8 (sc)
ISBN: 1-4259-0887-X (dj)

Library of Congress Control Number: 2005910882

Printed in the United States of America
Bloomington, Indiana

This book is printed on acid-free paper.

Bloomington, IN   Milton Keynes, UK

www.authorhouse.com

Acknowledgments

First off, I want to thank my high school sweetheart, and wife of more than 22 years, Susan. Susan, thank you for understanding my heart's desire for perfection, knowing all the while that I'm not perfect. What a wonderful journey this life with you has been so far. I pray we can walk together for many years to come.

I thank God for my children, Phillip, Lacey and Anthony. To you three, I dedicate my prayers and love. May God grant you a long, healthy life and may your walk be one of perfection in all you desire. To my immediate family, my mother, Evelyn Jo, and brother, Marty the drummer, thanks for your confidence in me. To my aunt and uncle, Janette and Tinsley, thank you for stepping in at a time when my father's health forced him to step out. You're the best!

To the clients of Walker Financial Services, thank you for your trust in me to be your guide. I commit to you my desire to help you in your walk in any way I can.

To The Strategic Coach Program™, for helping me to discover my "Unique Ablility®" and the importance of process. To Dan Taylor – my coach during The StrategicCoach Program – thank you for pushing me to write this book. You, along with all of the other mentors listed on the back of this book, have given me a new understanding of why it is so important to be associated with wise businessmen who want to do it right! And finally, to Mark Patterson, thank you for your patience and creative insight that enabled me to pull this book together. Without you, there's no way it could of have happened.

A special thank you to my deceased father, Dick Walker, whose humor and straight shooting manner influenced me greatly. Also, to my granddad, Bill Hardin, and his faithful wife, Hazel, who filled a tremendous void in my life during a time following the divorce of my parents. I will never forget you.

To my Saturday morning men's group, Don, Jay, Mike and Jase, thank you for your prayers and accountability each week. I am so fortunate to have met the four of you.

And finally, to God Himself, who by His grace and mercy, found me in the woods, put me on His holy path and has been guiding my walk home ever since. What an honor to wake each morning, knowing full well that You are here guiding me along. While I realize I'm not worthy, I am truly thankful.

Table of Contents

Foreword.. x

Step One
    Determine Your Level of Worry............................ 1

Step Two
    Create Your Own Retirement Vision...................... 16

Step Three
    Say Goodbye to Granddad's Retirement.................. 28

Step Four
    Know the Rules of the Game............................... 44

Step Five
    Admit You're Human.. 60

Step Six
    Take Responsibility... 83

Step Seven
    Work Hard (But Just Slow Down)......................... 105

Step Eight
    Have Fun (Just Be Sure To Bring Someone With You)..... 123

Step Nine
    Be Thankful... 146

Step Ten
    Trust God with the Rest..................................... 158

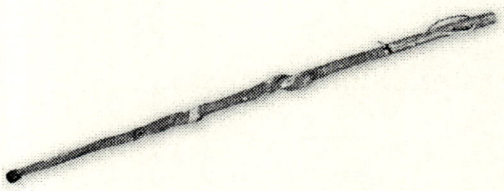

Foreword

While the destination of any journey is the primary goal, the journey itself often provides the true joy and meaning. The Perfecting Your Walk™ book series is about your walk, your life's journey. Because, life is not a marathon. It's not a 50-yard dash either. Your life is meant to be an enjoyable walk of discovery and happiness.

I want you to visualize your life as a walk through time. As with any journey in unfamiliar territory, you'll need a guide. Think of me as your guide. Together, we'll chart your course, blaze the trail, and set a pace that is comfortable for you. Whether you're retired, or planning for retirement, this book will help you gain a better understanding of the proper perspective and game plan needed to enjoy a WorryFree Retirement™.

Can you really have a WorryFree Retirement? Of course you can. So where do you start? Let's start with "worry."

Of the thousands of people I've spoken with, their biggest worry is the uncertainty of their future. This worry is really the symptom of a bigger problem – no clear vision of where they want to go in life. This lack of a direction leads them to wander and stumble, and the faster they go, the more lost they become. Out of desperation, they leave the path they're on, only to get lost deeper in the woods. Frantically, they search for shortcuts; get-rich-quick schemes, risky investments, and other unrealistic windfalls. This frantic pace only compounds the problem, increasing their level of worry even more. They max-out their WorryMeter. They reach the end of their rope. Does this sound like you? Are you stumbling, wandering or

Foreword

lost in the woods? Do you have a game plan that allows you to worry less about your money? Are you enjoying your walk through life?

Wherever you are, *10 Steps to a WorryFree Retirement* is for you. This book is more than just financial ideas and planning tips. It's a compass, complete with worksheets and an action planner, to help guide you in Perfecting Your Walk™. So grab your walking stick and let's get started.

*"As you walk
through life...*

*...remember that
the journey itself is just as important as the
destination."*

~ Tony Walker

WorryFree Retirement Guide Two-Minute Walk Exercises

To help you on your journey, we've included at the end of each step The WorryFree Retirement™ Two-Minute Walk Exercise. These unique exercises will pinpoint the areas which require your immediate attention. They will help you determine what's worrying you so you can do something about it. We all worry, and need a road map to keep us on course. That's what these exercises will do.

Of course, before starting any journey, you first must decide where you're going. While our destination is a WorryFree Retirement, the journey – enjoying life and money along the way – is just as important. Once you clarify the destination, the goals needed to get there will become clear and easier to achieve. Our WorryFree Retirement™ ActionPlanner, located at the end of the book, will allow you to summarize each Two-Minute Exercise into your Personal ActionPlan. As part of the process for dealing with worry, the ActionPlan will serve as a compass to monitor your progress. In order to make your walk even better, we've built the ActionPlanner as a two-seater, so you can bring someone along with you. That way, you won't feel like you're going it alone.

Step one

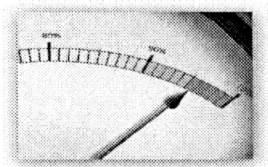

Determine Your Level Of Worry

"Worry is merely a symptom of a greater fear."

~ Tony Walker

Did you read in the paper recently where the government is working on a new device called The WorryMeter™?

You didn't hear about this?

While it's apparently still in the research stage, here's what the report says the government is planning on doing. Once approved, the WorryMeter will be issued to all Americans regardless of whether they work or are already retired. Everyone will be required to wear The WorryMeter each and every day, all day long. In fact, it will be strapped to our foreheads in plain view of everyone. The article I read went on to say The WorryMeter will be three inches high and four inches wide, with a big dial alternating between three color-shaded areas: green, yellow and red. This way, according to the government, everyone can monitor everyone else's level of worry by watching the dial move back and forth. With The WorryMeter, no one will be able to hide their worries. No more fudging on your tax return. No more lying to the police officer about going within the speed limit. No more faking it, when you should be making it. No more "I'm fine" after someone asks, "How are you doing?" Face it, we won't be able to hide anything from anybody anymore.

Of course, there is no such device…I just needed to get your attention. But let's think about this a minute. In today's culture, where we all want everyone else to think we are doing well, who in their right mind would walk around with such a device? If the government mandated that such a device be worn, they'd have Boston Tea Party II on their hands. No one would wear The WorryMeter because none of us would want others to see

Step One: Determine Your Level of Worry

how much we worry, especially when it comes to our worries and fears over our money issues – such as retirement.

The key word is *fear*. Worry is actually a symptom, and a warning sign, of fear. What kind of fear? Fear of the unknown or the unexpected...fear of running out of money...fear of another terrorist attack...fear of the stock market crashing...fear over debt...and on and on. We don't just fear things for no reason. Every fear, no matter how irrational it may seem, has a root cause. *(Even phobias, which can seem totally irrational, have some kind of root cause, perhaps buried deep in the phobic person's psyche.)* As for the everyday fears most of us have, the majority can be boiled down to that first fear I mentioned; fear of the unexpected or the unknown. Because we're human, we want to know what to expect in the future. That's only natural. Why do you think people today still pay good money to fortune tellers and palm readers? Because it's hard to predict the future (despite what all those TV "psychics" claim), we fear what might happen. And this fear makes us worry. In other words, we worry because we're human.

So what are you worried about right now? If you had The WorryMeter strapped to your forehead, what things in your life would send the arrow into the red zone? Your health, your kids, your jobs, your faith, your marriage, your money, your retirement? If you're still able to fog a mirror, chances are you're worried about something.

Perfecting Your Walk is all about worrying less and enjoying more. It's a philosophy that says: plan for tomorrow, but live for today. With so many Americans living for tomorrow and planning for today, Perfecting Your Walk comes at the right time. The purpose of this book is to deal with your worries head-on, rather than acting as if they will magically disappear.

Perfecting Your Walk begins by taking responsibility for your worries so you can get to the root of your fears. While our destination is based on our view of the future, we must never take for granted our daily walk – the journey.

Americans do worry about retirement. I hear it and see it in my practice every day. Yet the average consumer thinks he or she is the only one who is worried. That's because his or her neighbors are spending money as if it's growing on trees. But believe me, just because your neighbor appears to have his material act together, that doesn't mean he isn't worried. By the time you complete this book, you'll understand why.

To understand why so many people are worried about retirement, you have to go to the source of the problem – the tumor, if you will. Retirement is a man-made idea, proposed to Americans some 70 years ago. Prior to that time, there's no account of people sitting around planning to quit work, mow the lawn everyday and play golf for the rest of their lives.* People back then didn't worry about 401(k) plan balances, stock portfolios, mutual funds, and real estate investment trusts, because there was no need to. So what changed along the way?

We'll go in to more detail later on, but for now, let's just say that you don't have to buy into the modern-day notion of retirement. In fact, if this notion is creating worry, maybe it's time to create your own vision, which we'll show you how to do in the next chapter. But first things first, we need to determine your level of worry before we can find a cure for it. Here's the problem today, it all comes back to being human; and because we're human, we want what others want. We don't want to be the odd man out. If someone says we should stress over retirement, we stress. If the financial institutions and their "experts" representing them tell us we should have more money saved, we believe them and start worrying. Better yet, if these same folks can make us feel real guilty because we didn't plan well, that's all the more reason for us to start worrying.

Such logic backfires in most cases. I see people giving up on retirement because they lack trust in the people advising them. Just look at all of the discount brokers popping up. Folks feel that everybody wants their money, that the person or institution advising them is more interested in what they make on the deal versus what the client makes.

I suggest you try this little test on your advisor. Call them out of the blue and tell them you're pulling all of your money out of the account they manage. Wait for their response. If they act concerned for "you," then you've probably got a good person helping you. If, on the other hand, they get mad or even defensive that you would ever dream of taking "your" money from them, you may want to go ahead and get your money out of there as quickly as you can.

A sign that Americans are losing hope is found in the amount of consumer spending as compared to consumer saving. For most Americans, the outgo (spending) far exceeds the "in-go" (savings). When you have no clear vision of the future, no hope in what lies ahead, giving in and giving up are certainly two options you can choose. However, eventually either course of action will fail. You'll wake up one day more worried than before. Given the uncertainty over the future, it's easy to understand why Americans spend money they don't have, on things they don't need, to impress people they don't like anyway.

Feeling hopeless about today's version of retirement is a sign that you've bought into the myth of retirement. You've been sucked into someone else's vision for your life. When you're doing something you are uncomfortable with, such as following someone's advice you don't understand, you'll worry.

Couples of all ages attempt to control their future by controlling their money. It's an impossible task. There are too many variables to consider. Interest rates fluctuate, kids get sick, parents get sick, the market goes up, the market goes down, health care costs keep rising, and people don't know exactly when they are going to die. And today's baby boomers? Their money seems to disappear as fast they make it. Their 401(k) is less this year than it was three years ago, and the kids' college accounts have enough money to last about two semesters. Meantime, the group at or near retirement hasn't fared much better. While they have fixed income from pensions and social security, their savings accounts aren't keeping pace with inflation, IRA accounts consist of too much risk and no one has mapped out an exit strategy so they can use and enjoy their money.

That's why I created a process to help people create their own retirement vision. It's called The WorryFree Retirement™ Process. It establishes a game plan around your unique vision for the future. A Retirement Specialist trained in this process can now craft a personal game plan based on what you want, rather than what someone else says you should have.

Step One: Determine Your Level of Worry

No, the government isn't going to create a device to monitor your worry, but I did. And yes, it's called The WorryMeter. But unlike the one that would be strapped to your head for all to see, this WorryMeter is for your eyes only. It's simple and easy to use, and it will help get to the root of your worries so you can begin your own WorryFree Retirement. In order to determine your level of worry, you must be open and transparent about your fears and concerns. It works best when you bring along someone you trust – someone to confide in who can step back, see the path you are on, and then guide you back onto the right path for you. The problem is that nobody's comfortable talking about the things that worry them, especially when it comes to money. It's a very confidential subject. There can be a lot of guilt associated with having too much or having too little. Heck, people nowadays are more likely to tell you about their sex life before they'll tell you what's in their checking account. Maybe that's because people know more about sex than they do money.

Money is a difficult subject to discuss. And it doesn't help matters when "financial advisors/planners" make it even more complex. The typical advisor is not trained in the art of listening. They're trained in telling people "what" to do and "where" to invest. Their training (the same training I went through in my earlier years) doesn't teach them to explore the "wants" of the average consumer. The only folks they'll spend lots of time with are usually the super wealthy. But that probably doesn't help you. When I first got in this field, the extent of my training consisted in telling Joe Consumer "what" to do, rather than "how" to do it. As I read the emails from my TV show and speak in person with complete strangers who are worried about tomorrow, it is obvious that nothing has changed in the investment world. It's still the same old information. There are lots of opinions about "where" you should be putting your money, but there's never any discussion of "how" you should use and enjoy it in the safest manner possible. This lack of clear financial direction creates even more worry. Financial institutions and their advisors are another cause of worry. They have their own agendas, which usually involve pushing a specific product or products, rather than determining what is best for you as an individual. That's why a trained Retirement Specialist, independent of the financial institutions, is better suited in the "how." The definition of a Retirement Specialist is someone working for you, not someone else. Remember, it's your money, not theirs.

"But, Tony," you say, "I'm really not worried about my money or my retirement." To which I reply, "Then just wait." Worry is like the weather. One minute, the sky is clear blue, then, out of nowhere, a tsunami rolls in and sweeps you off your feet. Things hit us when we least expect it. Hopefully, this book will be a guide to handling the unexpected. You still won't be able to predict the future – no mere human can do that – but you will know you are doing everything you can to make that future as happy and fulfilling as possible for yourself and your loved ones. But the first thing you have to do is figure out your worry level. Once you gauge your level of worry, it's much easier to reduce it.

So let's begin our journey through a process of discovery. Let's make sure we know where you are, right now. The WorryMeter found at the end of this chapter is your tool. It was designed with you, the consumer, in mind. It has nothing to do with whether you should invest in stocks or bonds. It's much deeper and more important than products. It's about process. It's about you and your walk and what's worrying you. You're about to zero in on your biggest worry so you can focus your efforts and begin to make real progress toward your retirement vision.

However, we need to take it one step at a time. Don't get in a hurry. Trying to take on more than we're capable of only creates more worry. Don't think that doing more will get you there more quickly. The "busy-ness" trap can get you off track. You'll be less effective if you think this journey can be turned into a sprint. The WorryMeter is meant to slow you down, not speed you up. Since we'll be establishing a clearer vision of your future, you'll now be going somewhere at a pace that fits you and your philosophy.

Perfecting Your Walk is a new way of dealing with life's worry. Your journey should reflect who you are and where you wish to go in life. And finally, it should reflect how you wish to be remembered when this journey is complete. If you're not sure of your ultimate destination in life, don't worry, we'll help you clarify that. If you know, or think you know, the destination but feel you have no plan, stop worrying. We can give you the tools.

Please don't expect amazing things to happen overnight. It will take work and discipline. The philosophy of Perfecting Your Walk includes learning to work harder, yet slowing down. It teaches us to take our time and enjoy the pit stops of life. We begin to accept change, knowing nothing stays the same. We learn to embrace the plans we've made, but trust in others to help see them through. And before long, we find that we really are worrying less... and enjoying more.

Step One: Determine Your Level Of Worry

THE WORRYFREE RETIREMENT™ GUIDE: TWO-MINUTE WALK

The WorryMeter™ identifies your level of worry. This two-minute walk will help you uncover what's worrying you the most – right now. I'll be your guide throughout these exercises. As I mentioned at the beginning of this book, there will be similar exercises located at the end of each step. Simply circle your immediate response to each question and follow the trail from there. At the end of the exercise, select the one top worry, write it at the bottom of the exercise and then transfer your worry to ActionPlanner located on page 177 at the back of this book. So, grab your walking stick and let's go!

Step 1   Determine Your Level of Worry

I'M WORRIED...	Not Worried	Somewhat Worried	Very Worried
that I don't have a clear vision for my retirement.	1 2 3	4 5 6 7	8 9 10
that I will run out of money during retirement.	1 2 3	4 5 6 7	8 9 10
that I'm losing money because of unnecessary taxes and fees.	1 2 3	4 5 6 7	8 9 10
that I don't have a game plan in place.	1 2 3	4 5 6 7	8 9 10
that I've got too much money invested in the stock market.	1 2 3	4 5 6 7	8 9 10
that I'll make bad choices due to the conflicting financial advice I'm getting.	1 2 3	4 5 6 7	8 9 10
that my finances are disorganized.	1 2 3	4 5 6 7	8 9 10
that I'm spending too much money.	1 2 3	4 5 6 7	8 9 10
that I don't know the best way to communicate money issues with family.	1 2 3	4 5 6 7	8 9 10
that when I die, family members won't know how best to handle my estate.	1 2 3	4 5 6 7	8 9 10

MY BIGGEST WORRY IS...

_____

_____

(transfer to ActionPlanner on page 177)

Step Two

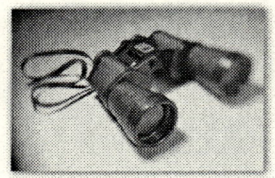

Create Your Own Retirement Vision

"The key to catching fish is to keep your eye on the fish, not the other fishermen." ~Anonymous

It's been said that vision without action is a daydream, and action without vision is but a nightmare. Creating a WorryFree Retirement™ begins by first clarifying your vision of retirement. Unfortunately, most folks never do this. If you are worried about retirement, chances are you have no vision of what it is you really want. If you don't have a clear vision of where you are going, it's due to one of two reasons: you don't care, or nobody has coached you in how to create and establish a vision. Since you're reading this book, I will assume that you do care and that you are open to a little coaching. Fair enough?

Step Two: Create Your Own Vision

There are three key ingredients necessary to reaching your destination. Before getting started you must:

1. Determine your "ideal" vision and then write it down. If it's not written down in a place where you can go and review it regularly (yes, even if it's memorized in your mind's eye), then it's not a serious goal to begin with. So let's try it now. In the space provided below, simply write your "ideal" retirement. Keep it short and simple (twenty words or less):

_____

_____

_____

_____

2. Assuming you've written down your "ideal" vision for retirement, the next key step is to "Commit" to the vision by sharing it with someone whom you trust who will monitor your progress along the way. So let's think of one person whom you trust. It could be your spouse, a friend, your advisor; just think about a person that has your best interest

at heart. Someone who cares about you and your well-being. Write their name here:

_____

_____

3. Set up a plan of action, based on your current strengths, weaknesses, opportunities and threats to the vision. The ActionPlan must be flexible to meet changes in the future. Now, this is where it gets a little tricky. It's not that simple, is it? Where do you begin setting up an ActionPlan? We'll help you by summarizing each and transferring our worries to page 177. For now, though, let's keep walking.

Most Americans are a fairly educated bunch. From the time our parents are comfortable putting us on a school bus and shipping us off for the day, we are exposed to a wide variety of subjects. Yet, few students ever receive an education in "goal setting." That's because educators don't know anything about the subject. We're asked what we want to be when we grow up, and that's about it. No one asks us to think about who we

Step Two: Create Your Own Vision

are and where we want to be in life. The only time teachers mention the word "walk" is when you're told to walk, not run through the halls.

Few people have a clear vision of their future – including their financial future – because no one has coached them through the process of goal setting. You sure can't depend on the representatives of the financial institutions.

But that's hardly surprising. Their job, after all, is not to help you clarify your vision, but to simply gather your money. They take your money, shuffle it around like a deck of cards, and then somehow "they" always come out on top. Even in the mutual fund industry, while your funds go down, the financial advisors still get paid (in the form of asset fees). Ultimately you are left standing at the end of the line, waiting for something in return. Banks, Insurance Companies, Mutual Funds – they're all in the game of making money on your money. That's all they do, and they know what they're doing (ever see a bank go out of business in your hometown?). This is why they never talk to you about clarifying your vision for retirement. There's nothing in it for them. To more fully understand why advisors neglect this aspect of planning, let's revisit this whole notion of retirement and how it all got started.

Back in the 1930s, our country was in the middle of the Great Depression. People weren't working and making money because there were few jobs to be had. This Depression left Americans with little to hope for. So the government stepped in and introduced the Social Security System in 1935; as part of the " New Deal." Social Security was created with the best of intentions. It was the government's way of creating a safety net for widows, orphans and retirees.

By the way, America didn't invent Social Security; it was actually started by a German fellow by the name of Otto von Bismarck. Perhaps you've heard of him? Back in the 1800s, Bismarck realized that the young folks of Germany needed something to do – work. But since there were no jobs, the German government came up with the idea of giving benefits to the older Germans in exchange for their quitting work. This way, jobs would open up for the younger fellows, and the younger fellows would pay taxes on their wages to keep the older guys retired. Pretty simple, huh?

Fast forward to the 1930s in America. The U.S. was in financial trouble so some of the powers-that-were thought Bismarck's idea was a good way to give Americans hope.

Contrary to popular opinion, however, Social Security was not a universally accepted concept in 1935. Some people considered it a form of socialism, whereby the government took from some and gave to others. This issue was hotly debated. Conservatives were very skeptical of the government offering such a program. Most people back then felt, as some people still feel today, that the government should stay out of the financial planning business. Many feared that a program such as Social Security would make people too dependent upon the government, thereby giving the Feds more power than the founders of our country ever intended. These were, and are, valid concerns. Nevertheless, the 1930s were desperate times, and Social Security was a product of that desperation. The Social Security Act was introduced, accepted and put into law.

Since that time, the U.S. has never looked back, but it also appears that no one wants to look forward. Once again we are in desperate times, but the nature of that desperation has changed since the '30s. There are far more people, living much longer lives, and our material expectations have gone way up. We have built an entire culture on expectations that simply are not sustainable under the current system. Today, politicians are finally beginning to admit doubts about Social Security working effectively in the future. I believe that the Social Security system will eventually become a welfare-type system. It will benefit only the people who qualify based on their income and other financial factors. This is very similar to what has happened to other programs, such as Medicaid. They start out for everyone, but eventually the government cannot afford to cover everyone. The math never works.

Here's the math behind Social Security as we know it, and why it's doomed for failure. As more and more people retire, there are going to be less and less people to support the system. In order for the Social Security system to remain solvent, taxes (in-go) must be increased or benefits (outgo) must be reduced.

These are our only two options and Americans do not seem to want either one. We all seem to want to have our cake and eat it too. That just isn't possible.

Let's get back to the concept of "retirement." Just whose idea was it to convince hardworking people to pick some magical age in the future, quit work and retire to play golf, mow the lawn, travel and walk around the local mall every morning? Who came up with the idea of convincing people to stockpile large sums of money in hopes of living off of it for the rest of their lives? Well, to understand the problem, we need to go back once again to the beginning of Social Security.

Back in the 1930s, the government never dreamed that so many people would even reach 65, much less live past that ripe old age. In 1935, the average life expectancy in the US (for both sexes) was 61.7 years. The life expectancy for men was 59.9, and for women 63.9. So age 65 was deemed the magical time when people would quit going to work every day; instead they would go to the mail box every month to get their Social Security check. The government just never figured on the possibility that someday, medical advancements would keep so many people alive far past the age of 65. That's why the system is in trouble. Today's worker is contributing to a system that immediately pays his or her contribution out to current retirees. With all the new money simply going to pay the benefits of today's retirees, there is no real savings or "lock-box" within the system. Those in the 1930s who objected to the idea of Social Security were right – politicians make lousy financial planners.

In all fairness, the system worked well for a few decades. Granddad never had to worry about Social Security. When he walked to the mailbox on the first of each month, his Social Security check was there. Granddad invested in the system, and got his fair share in return. Today, however, there's no guarantee that some Americans will ever receive any of our money back from Social Security.

This reality check regarding the Social Security system may not cure your worry, but it should help you to understand one of the causes of it. Social Security is not the only cause, of course. You'll soon see why most financial institutions make lousy planners as well. Their ability to predict the future is no more accurate than the politicians of the 30s.

That's why casting your own vision for retirement is so important. A clear vision will give you more confidence to plan for the future. Being armed with your own clear vision – a vision which is going to be based on who you are and what you want in life – will allow you to stay focused. It will allow you to stay on track and be less dependent on the opinions and assumptions of other financial guides. Establishing a focused game plan will allow you to control your money so you can worry less about it.

Step Two: Create Your Own Retirement Vision

THE WORRYFREE RETIREMENT™ GUIDE: TWO-MINUTE WALK

Creating a powerful and compelling vision for the future helps you to focus on what matters most in your life. I will guide you through this two-minute exercise so you can more clearly describe your most fundamental goals and aspirations for your life. This exercise will forget the fact that the government and financial institutions cannot help you chart the course. You will have to determine your own destination in life before you can begin the journey. Remember, the journey is just as important as the destination itself.

Step 2 Create Your Own Retirement Vision

I'M WORRIED...	Not Worried	Somewhat Worried	Very Worried
that my vision for retirement is vague and difficult to communicate with others.	1 2 3	4 5 6 7	8 9 10
that I won't be able to travel as much as I'd like to.	1 2 3	4 5 6 7	8 9 10
that I won't be able to give as much as I'd like to.	1 2 3	4 5 6 7	8 9 10
that I won't have the resources to enjoy a hobby or special interest.	1 2 3	4 5 6 7	8 9 10
that I won't be able to spend time with family.	1 2 3	4 5 6 7	8 9 10
that my finances will be disorganized and scattered everywhere.	1 2 3	4 5 6 7	8 9 10
that my money isn't safely invested.	1 2 3	4 5 6 7	8 9 10
that I'll have to continue working long into retirement.	1 2 3	4 5 6 7	8 9 10
that I will not be able to maintain the same lifestyle as I currently enjoy.	1 2 3	4 5 6 7	8 9 10
that I might become financially dependent on others.	1 2 3	4 5 6 7	8 9 10

MY BIGGEST WORRY IS...

_____

_____

(transfer to ActionPlanner on page 177)

Step Three

Say Goodbye To Granddad's Retirement

"Nothin' stays the same." ~ Tony's father

Were you close to your Granddad? I was. As a young lad, I spent a great deal of time with him. He lived in small community called Troy, just outside Lexington, Kentucky. Because my granddad was so laid back, my Uncle Eddie (his son) referred to the area where he lived as "the land of do as you please." My Granddad's retirement looked something like this: Granddad gets married and goes to work for a big company. Granddad works very hard at this big company, puts in his 43 years (with the same company), retires, and lives off the company pension plan for the rest of his life.

Step Three: Say Goodbye to Granddad's Retirement

At the magical age of 65, Granddad retires from the big company. The big company holds a nice retirement party for Granddad. Granddad brings home a nice clock and a plaque for all of his years of service. More importantly, along with his social security check, Granddad knows that a fat pension check will come in the mail every month until he and Grandma (Hazel) die. Granddad smiles, retires and goes home, calling it quits. His life consists of tinkering around the house, smoking cigarettes, drinking lots of coffee and religiously watching episodes of *The Tonight Show With Johnny Carson*. He and Hazel (Haz for short), have a steady income for the rest of their lives.

Their "mailbox" money, covered all of their daily expenses. His health insurance was still covered by his former employer. Granddad didn't need much else because there wasn't a lot of luxury involved in his lifestyle. He and Hazel didn't spend much money. Their guaranteed income stream took care of everything. Their vision of retirement was simple; enjoy the rest of their life in Troy. Other than going "to town" once a week to visit the grocery store, I never remember them venturing much outside of Troy. They certainly never took trips and vacations to exotic places. They lived a very humble lifestyle and their lives were quite predictable.

While I was around Granddad, I never heard him talk much about money. Actually, the only time I heard Granddad complain about money was when my brother and I would run up the driveway to the country store and buy candy and soft drinks. We'd load up on junk, walk up to the counter of the store, and confidently say, "Just put it on Granddad's tab."

Both of my grandparents are now deceased. They lived less than 20 years past the age of 65. They're dead and gone – and so is this type of retirement for most Americans. Face it; the predictable days of Granddad's retirement are over! As I implied in the previous chapter, more than likely, there will be no "mailbox" money for you and me.

So let's look at today's retirement situation. Because people are living longer, they're going to need their money to last a whole lot longer than Granddad's did. Today, a retirement age of 65 may not be realistic. Granddad had guaranteed Social

Step Three: Say Goodbye to Granddad's Retirement

Security and pension checks coming in each month. What will you have? Granddad had a relatively "worry-free" retirement. Alas, the pension plan of Granddad's day went the way of the dinosaur. And Social Security, well, we've already discussed the reality of that system.

If you want to retire like Granddad, you'll need boat loads of money to create your own pension income, because you're not going to get it from anybody else. For example: Let's say you have $500,000 in your retirement account. This could be your 401(k), IRA, whatever. Keep in mind that the same politicians who created these plans will probably take a bunch of it away when you retire. It's called taxes. Depending on your overall net worth, they have the right to take as much as 80% of it! In other words, the money you saved into these 401(k) type plans gave you a pre-tax deduction. That's a good thing. The drawback to a "pre-tax" deduction is that you have pay taxes on every penny when you go to spend it...that's a bad thing.

But let's say you could make an average of 5% (please forget those 10% returns, most investors don't acheive them) on this $500,000 account. In other words, you retire, take the $500,000 that was in your 401(k) plan, roll it into an IRA and invest it for an average return of 5% for the rest of your life. Let's further assume that you and your spouse live 30 years past retirement – which is very possible nowadays. After a careful retirement analysis, we determine that the two of you need $40,000 a year to live on. Keep in mind that that $40,000 of income must increase each year just to keep pace with inflation. I generally like to assume an inflation rate of 4%. In other words, if you need $40,000 this year, then based on 4% inflation, you will need $41,600 next year (4% of $40,000 is an extra $1,600 you'll need next year).

Given all of these variables, and based on a 5% after-tax rate of return we're speaking of, you would run out of money at age 79. That's right; at age 79, based on these assumptions, you're now officially broke. That's not what I would call a WorryFree Retirement™ plan.

Step Three: Say Goodbye to Granddad's Retirement

Pension plans were great for Granddad, but if you're a baby boomer, forget it. A pension income was a huge security blanket for Granddad, but it's going to be a distant memory for most of us. Without the guaranteed pension plan, employees are now being offered what's called a 401(k) plan. The 401(k) plan is a poor substitute for the pension plan. It has no resemblance to a pension plan whatsoever. A 401(k) plan is merely a way for you to set aside money in a retirement account on a pre-tax basis. Unfortunately, with most people putting their 401(k) balances into growth mutual funds and other risky investments, they have no future security. Rather than having a guaranteed pension like Granddad, you're now being encouraged by the financial institutions to put your retirement money at risk. And the employer? The only skin they have in the game is to simply "match" a portion of your 401(k) contribution. And this "match" is voluntary. Your employer isn't required to invest their money in your 401(k) plan. It's now all up to you.

Another issue that concerns Americans is the cost of health care. My granddad had all of his health care needs taken care of by his employer. When he retired, they kept his health insurance in force and paid all of the premiums. This probably won't be the case for you and me. With health care costs spiraling out of control, are you prepared to pay for it? Whether health care is a right or a privilege for everyone will not be debated in this book. The fact is, everyone expects good health care. The question is, who's going to pay for it? And with people living longer, we can only assume that health care costs will continue to go up.

In Granddad's day, folks didn't worry so much about their health. They only visited the doctor when they had serious medical issues. There were few diagnostic tools available. Even if a serious medical problem was discovered, the medical technology to cure the problem may not have existed. People in Granddad's day got old (if they were lucky) and eventually dropped dead. Today, medical advancements allow people to hang around for years, only to finally end up in some nursing home for the rest of their life. That's another ironic worry created by longer life expectancies. Preventive medicine back in Granddad's day was minimal at best. I can't even remember my grandparents taking prescription medications. Now the average person I meet in their '70s spends $200-$500 per month on prescription medication. Today, living longer creates more worry. We're faced with higher medical costs and less money to cover them.

And what about your standard of living as compared to Granddad? When I visit with people from the World War II generation, these folks are amazed at how younger people spend money today. They can't understand why their kids are already more affluent (from a materialistic standpoint) than they are. Granddad's generation hated debt; society today can't get enough of it. Seniors I meet with truly worry how their kids and grandkids will retire when so much money is being spent rather than invested.

So what's the problem with today's notion of retirement? The advertisers and financial institutions try to convince you to spend and enjoy your money and retire at age 55. In other words, all of this can be yours if you'll just give us your money. Don't worry, be happy. Go ahead, purchase a really nice home (or two), travel the world and spend your money however you want to spend it. We'll be there to take care of you with our 20% returns and wishful thinking.

You can't have it both ways. If you're going to spend and enjoy your money (which is okay by me) then you'll have to work longer than you think (which is also okay by me). However, if you really wish to retire someday, you can't be spending your money and blindly throwing the rest into the world of stocks and growth mutual funds, thinking this will be your savior. That's not investing, that's speculating!

As I see the big picture, most of you are not going to be able to retire like this. Oh, sure, you can retire, but you'll run out of money. That's because you have no financial game plan. Unlike Granddad's retirement, your game plan may have to include working long past the age of 65 in order to support such a lifestyle. As you get older, you're going to need more and more money. Because you'll live longer than Granddad, the impact of inflation will catch up with you. A free-spending lifestyle won't help matters either.

Step Three: Say Goodbye to Granddad's Retirement

Today, people's retirement expectations (speculation) are loftier than Granddad's were. They forget how expensive things will be. Just put yourself to the test right now. Look around your house and compare what you have versus what Granddad had. Imagine Granddad rising out of his grave and coming over to your house to check out your lifestyle. Can you imagine his eyes bugging out, wondering how in the world you could afford all that you have?

Finally, Granddad never worried about the cost of technology. While technology is good, it comes at a huge cost to your retirement. Technology changes so quickly, which means you have to replace gadgets and gizmos more frequently. Change is always expensive. Granddad never spent money on CDs, DVDs, computers, MP3s, cell phones, PDAs, plasma TVs... the list of gadgets goes on and on. And so does the cost.

When I was a kid in the 1960s, gadgets and gizmos didn't exist, at least not nearly to the extent that they do today. Granddad's house had only one television and one telephone. Both were located in the family room. There was no cable TV, it was free, compliments of an antenna which was perched on the roof of every home in Troy. Granddad received three channels. If the weather turned nasty, forget it. And there were certainly no PlayStations to contend with. Oh, and one more thing – I know bathrooms don't fall in the gadgets- and- gizmos category, but Granddad's house only had one "reading room" located beside the kitchen (lucky for us plenty of air freshener was on hand). My guess is that even if all those neat toys I mentioned had existed in Granddad's day, he wouldn't have wanted them – mainly because he couldn't have afforded them. Back then, if you didn't have the cash, you didn't get it. There were no such things as credit cards. There was credit, but it wasn't over-used and abused the way it is today. The only credit Granddad had was something called layaway! Layaway was an "easy payment" plan whereby the store put your merchandise aside, and you made regular payments until you had paid in full. Then, and only then, were you allowed to take the merchandise home and actually use it. Although it was a form of delayed gratification – a concept that's alien to many of us today, the upside was that you didn't spend a year or two or more paying for something that you'd grown sick of after having it for only a month!

Step Three: Say Goodbye to Granddad's Retirement

Owning several expensive cars wasn't Granddad's idea of a WorryFree Retirement either. I'm reminded of this whenever I visit my mother in Lexington. She still lives in the same house I grew up in. When our family goes to visit her, the kids are amazed at the narrowness of the driveway. It's about seven feet wide, as are all the other driveways on her street. The home was built in the 1940s, when the vast majority of people owned only one car. There was no reason for builders to consider a 40-foot-wide driveway leading up to a three-car garage. Yes, our lifestyles have ratcheted up quite a bit since Granddad's day.

So you can see why retiring like Granddad is going to be difficult, if not impossible. His lifestyle required a lot less money than ours. My advice: Decide right now what it is you really want out of life. Forget Granddad's retirement and forget the modern-day notion of it as well. It's up to you to create a much more realistic expectation of your options for a WorryFree Retirement. You cannot base your options on Granddad's retirement, nor can you base it on the modern-day "have your cake and eat it too" version. Your vision of retirement must be modified and constantly monitored by someone who understands the many changes that lie ahead. The Retirement Specialist you choose to work with must also be able to identify strengths, weaknesses, opportunities and threats to your retirement vision. Otherwise, you'll worry.

If I could sum up the point of this chapter – and, in fact, one of the main points of this whole book – it would be with three bits of wisdom that too many people have learned the hard way:

1. Count the cost!

2. Expect change.

3. Remember, a dollar today will be worth less tomorrow.

With those three tidbits in mind, you need to decide right now if there's any way you can live in comfort if you keep on doing things the way you are doing them. Decide today that comfort can be yours. But it must be defined and measured in realistic terms, and only you can do that (perhaps with the help of a qualified specialist). It's your retirement your vision, so you need to see the future through your own set of eyes, not through the eyes of others. Realize that it is your responsibility to decide how and when to retire, and exactly what that retirement will look like. You will need a guide to help you. But make sure the guide is familiar with the road ahead. Make sure the guide has the experience to help you set a safe and secure game plan so that you can accomplish your goals for the future.

Step Three: Say Goodbye To Granddad's Retirement

THE WORRYFREE RETIREMENT™ GUIDE: TWO-MINUTE WALK

Outdated ideas and perceptions of what Granddad's retirement looked like should be a distant memory now. Today, you must recognize the possibilities that lie ahead and learn to take advantage of them. To do that, you must recognize the differences between Granddad's retirement and your retirement. You must realize that while financial institutions and their advisors want and need your money, they shouldn't get it unless it fits within your vision — your game plan. This two-minute exercise will help you identify those differences so you can begin to set an action plan to deal with them.

Step 3 Say Goodbye to Granddad's Retirement

I'M WORRIED...	Not Worried	Somewhat Worried	Very Worried
that the stock market is more uncertain today.	1 2 3	4 5 6 7	8 9 10
that I'm not saving enough money.	1 2 3	4 5 6 7	8 9 10
that I'm spending too much money.	1 2 3	4 5 6 7	8 9 10
that I'll live much longer than Granddad.	1 2 3	4 5 6 7	8 9 10
that health care costs will skyrocket.	1 2 3	4 5 6 7	8 9 10
that I'm getting confused over the many investment options available.	1 2 3	4 5 6 7	8 9 10
that the government will continue to make taxes more confusing.	1 2 3	4 5 6 7	8 9 10
that I won't be able to rely on Social Security and/or pension plans.	1 2 3	4 5 6 7	8 9 10
that my current retirement accounts won't be enough.	1 2 3	4 5 6 7	8 9 10
that my financial advisor is not really working in my best interest.	1 2 3	4 5 6 7	8 9 10

MY BIGGEST WORRY IS...

_____

_____

(transfer to ActionPlanner on page 177)

Step Four

Know The Rules Of The Game

"If everybody played by the rules, we wouldn't need referees." ~ Tony Walker

Ever play chess?

It's a fairly straightforward game. The first player to capture his opponent's King, wins. To win at chess there are two simple rules one should follow. Rule number one: don't allow your opponent to capture your Queen. Rule number two: don't move your King unless you absolutely have to.

Step Four: Know the Rules of the Game

Since there are only two players, winning should not be too difficult. At least there's a 50% chance of winning, right? Each player knows the rules, has the same number of pieces at the start of the game, and is playing on the same board. What's to know!

As a kid, I remember playing chess with my older brother Marty. Not once do I remember beating him at chess. Granted, he was three years older than me, but hey, I was a fairly sharp, competitive kid in those days. So why did I always lose? Because, I didn't take time to "understand" the rules behind chess. What I failed to realize is that knowing the rules is one thing, understanding the importance of them is quite another. My philosophy back then was play hard and fast. In fact, during the first part of the game, my aggressive style of play led me to capture more of Marty's pieces. I'd capture a few pawns, maybe a bishop or knight, and because I had more pieces on the board than Marty, I thought I was winning.

I've discovered the game of life (and money) to be like chess. Think about it...we all start out with the same pieces, on the same board, armed with the same rules. However, most of us never understand the "strategy" behind the game. We play as hard and as fast as we can. Our strategy appears to be working. We collect a bunch of "pieces" and think we're winning. Our King and Queen appear to be safe so we stay the course: seek and destroy. Never mind that in the meantime, our opponent is systematically and methodically moving his pieces as if we are not even playing the same game. Seeing our rapid progress toward our goal and seemingly getting closer to capturing his King, we become overly confident, paying less attention to the details of the game. Then, out of nowhere, our opponent grabs our Queen (we break rule number one). Quickly, other pieces begin to fall into his hands. We realize we're in trouble, but we have no exit strategy. Worry sets in thinking we're going to lose. We realize we aren't in control any longer. Out of desperation, we do the unthinkable; we begin moving our King (just broke the second rule). Of course, the game's over. He wins - you lose.

When it comes to playing the money game, there are two "Golden Rules." The first, Golden Rule of money says: "The one who knows the rules, gets the gold." The other Golden Rule: "The one who makes the rules, keeps the gold!" If you're going to play to win, you better know the rules. Unfortunately, most people never take the time to learn them.

To help you understand the retirement rules, we'll examine another game – basketball. Just like chess, basketball is pretty simple. The object of basketball is to score more points than your opponent. Unlike chess, where there is no time clock and time could play forever waiting for someone to run out of money, basketball is more like life – it has a time clock. The game is divided in to three parts: the first half, halftime, and the second half. Let's take a look at each half, and compare it to "real life."

<u>First half strategy in basketball</u>: Start with a game plan devised by your coach, based on what he knows about your opponent. Take your game out on the floor, play as hard as you can and try to score as many points as possible. Size up the opponent, make adjustments, keep an eye on the scoreboard and try to stay ahead. The scoreboard tells you how well you are doing.

First half strategy in life: Get a job, find a coach (advisor), work as hard as you can (score points) and save a little money. Spend the rest trying to raise your family, keep your opponents (IRS, brokerage and bank fees, insurance premiums, market losses, inflation) from taking the ball away from you. Watch the scoreboard (investment statements, 401(k) balances, debt) to see if you're winning or losing the game. The first half of life is what I call the "accumulation" phase.

Halftime strategy in basketball: Run to the locker room and take a breather. Allow the coach time to assess the game. Discover new things about your opponent you didn't expect. Make substitutions in players if necessary. Try to take out the biggest player on the opponent's team (don't let him get the ball near the basket) so he won't beat you.

Halftime strategy in life: Run to the locker room to meet with your coach (advisor). Realize where you stand according to the scoreboard (your investment statements and debts). "Accumulate" as much money as you can. Take the extra money you have due to higher wages, (and maybe your kids being out of the house), and stockpile that away as well. Don't get frustrated if you are behind. Begin a plan which includes reducing risk over time. Take time to ask your coach some questions about his or her strategy for helping you enjoy this money. Find out if the coach is a trained "accumulation" specialist (only concerned with points on the scoreboard) or a "distribution" specialist (concerned with assisting you in a plan to enjoy your money). Try to take out the biggest player on the opponent's team so he won't beat you (reduce taxes on your assets and income for instance).

<u>Second half strategy in basketball</u>: Put your best foot forward, knowing the clock is ticking. Don't get in a hurry. Listen to the coach if he knows what he's doing (you can look at the scoreboard and tell). Minimize your mistakes, as there is less time to go back and recover. Play good defense and execute the strategy your coach created during half time. Don't get into foul trouble or you'll lose your best player. And above all else, when the game gets tight and it's coming down to the wire, don't listen to the crowd. Stay focused on the main goal; scoring more points than your opponent.

<u>Second half strategy in life</u>: Put your best foot forward, knowing the clock is ticking (the game will end when you die). Don't get in a hurry (you should be encouraged by your progress if you have a clear vision of where you are going). Listen to the coach if he knows what he's doing (or, since it's your money, you can always fire the coach if he doesn't know what he's doing; you can look at the scoreboard and tell). Minimize your mistakes (take less risk with your money) as there is less time to go back and recover. Play good defense (minimize unnecessary taxes and fees on your money) and execute the strategy your coach created during half time (use and enjoy your money). Don't get into foul trouble (having unrealistic expectations of how and when you can retire), or you will lose your best player. And above all else, when the game gets tight and it's coming down to the wire, don't listen to the crowd (the guy who tells you to hang in there when your account drops by 50%). Stay focused on the main goal: creating a WorryFree Retirement based on your vision, not someone else's.

Just as you need a good game plan to win at basketball, to create a WorryFree Retirement, you must have a well thought out game plan. The financial industry doesn't understand how to do this. They only look at the first half, and they look only at the scoreboard. That's the only means of monitoring your progress. They never create strategies to beat your opponent. A WorryFree Retirement game plan includes a realistic view and understanding of the game being played. There may come a day during your retirement when the worry overcomes you, and things appear hopeless. I've met many retirees who feel this way. The reason they feel hopeless is that they think it's too late. The world is telling them they had their chance during the first half. Even their coach won't take any blame. He'll just say, "you knew the risk of the game."

So where are you in life? Even if you're in the second half, there's still hope. The second half of your life is what I call the "distribution phase." The distribution phase is serious business. This is where a game plan will either pass or fail. The plans you put in place during the first half will determine whether you will enjoy a WorryFree Retirement™ and how much you can use during the second half.

Unfortunately, most financial advisors, and the institutions they represent, have a conflict of interest during the second half of your life. As much as they say you can use and enjoy your money during retirement, you really can't. That's because if you actually take the money back from them, they will lose it and the interest on it. This goes against their Golden Rule. They can't make money unless they have your money. If you take your money back to use and enjoy, they lose control and you win the game.

Accumulating money is important, but learning how to use and enjoy it is the key to life. A true financial game plan is one that allows you to do both. Accumulate money on a safe basis and distribute it out on a safe basis over the rest of your life.

So whether you're in the first half of life (trying to accumulate as much money as possible), at half time (getting close to retirement and starting to think seriously about it), or in the second half of life (officially retired and trying to figure out how to live off the money you've accumulated), remember that financial institutions are under no obligation to coach you how to win. They aren't going to teach you the rules either.

Let's take a real-life example of first half (accumulation planning) with no second half (distribution) strategy in mind. We will examine the ever-popular 401(k) plan. The 401(k) plan is a tax-qualified plan, meaning that the money you invest goes into the plan on a pre-tax basis, but taxed when you take it out.

For instance: Joe Worker makes $50,000 per year. His employer-sponsored 401(k) plan allows him to put in $5,000 toward the plan. Joe's $5,000 goes in on a pre-tax basis, meaning Joe doesn't have to pay income taxes on the full $50,000. Instead, he gets to subtract the $5,000 off the top. Now he's only taxed on $45,000. This is good news, because Joe doesn't pay taxes on the money as it goes into the plan. That's good first-half planning. The bad news is that during the second half of life, every penny Joe pulls out will be taxed! Not only will it be taxed, but it will be taxed at whatever tax rate Joe's in at the time he retires. Given the problems the U.S. government is having right now, do you want to guess whether tax rates will be higher or lower 20-30 years from now? My guess is they'll be higher. So the government gets their money one way or another. A 401(k) plan merely "postpones" taxes, it doesn't save taxes. Sooner or later, Joe's got to pay up.

Advisors who happen to work for the investment companies holding your 401(k) money tell you to fund your 401(k) to the "max." They have no interest in showing you how to use and enjoy it. Investment companies love 401(k) plans. They get to keep and hold all of that money and draw fees on it. You, on the other hand, lose control of it.

In the meantime, Joe's employer is under no obligation to put money away for him. They have no skin in the game, as they say. The 401(k) plan is a good savings tool, but it's not going to make the average person wealthy. In fact, most 401(k) plan balances have not increased in value over the last several years, due to the down turn in the stock market. That's just one more reason you shouldn't have so much of your money tied up in growth mutual funds inside the 401(k) plan. Be very wary of doing this.

So let's take a walk through your "accumulation" phase with the 401(k) plan. Let's say you're ready to retire. You're age 65 and you've accumulated $500,000 in your plan. You go to your employer and ask if they could help you plan this 401(k) so that you can use and enjoy it. Since your employer is not even allowed to give you advice, they more than likely will simply give you a clock or plaque or whatever they're giving out these days, and tell you, "Good luck." You're given a toll-free number to call. You call the toll free number and discuss your retirement options with the rep who answers. The first and foremost thing on this rep's mind is making sure that this money stays with the institution. How do I know this? Because in my practice, we transfer money out of 401(k) plans into rollover IRAs all the time. I call the 1-800 numbers for my clients (with the client sitting there with me, of course). I always get a kick out of the person's reaction on the other end of the phone: they are simply shocked that anyone (my client) would consider moving "their money" away from the investment company representing the 401(k) plan.

The reality is, you need a retirement coach during the second half of life. A 1-800 number won't cut it. You need a Retirement Specialist who will sit down, face-to-face, and discuss your options and plans – someone who is trained in both accumulation and distribution planning.

"But Tony, I'm already retired," you're saying. "Most of my money is tied up in the stock market. That's what my stock broker and everybody else says I should be doing. They just keep telling me to hang in there whenever the market goes down. They keep telling me that the market goes down but it always comes back up – that in the long run, the market has done much better than any other investment. Are these people lying?"

They're not lying; they're just not telling you the whole truth. The market does eventually go up. But that doesn't mean you'll make money in the market. There are too many factors involved to simply make a blanket statement like that. In fact, if you take out the go-go 90s, it's estimated that the actual return of the stock market has been around 7%. The average investor has not done as well as the market. That's because the returns of the stock market reflect average returns over a period of time. This is a complicated way of saying that your particular investments, and the time when you were in the market, have a great deal to do with your personal returns. Historically speaking, the average investor has just not done very well in the stock market, based on these timing issues. No one can time the stock market, and it's not realistic to just look at average returns and assume that's what you're going to get. It's not that simple.

Investing for the future is just like in any ball game; you've got to pace yourself to win. Stick with your game plan and be ready to make adjustments over time. This is the key to success.

Step Four: Know The Rules Of The Game

THE WORRYFREE RETIREMENT™ GUIDE: TWO-MINUTE WALK

All good coaches know how essential it is to understand the strengths and weaknesses of themselves and their opponent. Knowing the rules of the game is your ally. Gaining a better understanding of how others make money on your money, and why they give the advice they do, will help filter out all the crowd noise so you can stay on course with your original vision. This exercise will help you determine what mistakes you might be making right now. Its intention is to call into question current things you might be doing that may or may not be good for you, depending on the "half" you are playing in.

Step 4 Know the Rules of the Game

I'M WORRIED...

	Not Worried	Somewhat Worried	Very Worried
that I'm putting too much money in my 401(k) plan.	1 2 3	4 5 6 7	8 9 10
that too much of my money is in taxable investments.	1 2 3	4 5 6 7	8 9 10
that I don't have a strategy for using and enjoying my 401(k) and/or IRA.	1 2 3	4 5 6 7	8 9 10
that I am making costly mistakes with my investments - and don't know it.	1 2 3	4 5 6 7	8 9 10
that nobody is competent to help me save on taxes during retirement.	1 2 3	4 5 6 7	8 9 10
that financial institutions know the rules better than I do.	1 2 3	4 5 6 7	8 9 10
that I won't be able to afford life insurance during retirement.	1 2 3	4 5 6 7	8 9 10
that I don't have the proper legal documents in place when I die.	1 2 3	4 5 6 7	8 9 10
that family members will be burdened with complicated rules at my death.	1 2 3	4 5 6 7	8 9 10
that the amount of my debts will reduce my retirement savings and income.	1 2 3	4 5 6 7	8 9 10

MY BIGGEST WORRY IS...

_____

_____

(transfer to ActionPlanner on page 177)

Admit You're Human

"The reason we hate to admit we're human, is because we are human." ~ Tony Walker

As human beings, we're all born dreamers. Over time, though, the reality of the world wakes us up from our dream-like state, hurling us into a state of constant nightmares. Running out of money, not being able to provide for family, outrageous health care costs, too many gadgets and gizmos – sometimes, we just wish we could turn off the lights and go back to sleep. But we can't, because the reality of life keeps us up at night (I refer to this as one's "sleep factor"). What begins as a pleasant dream during the first half of life – the idea of retiring in comfort like the couples in the magazine ads – quickly spirals out of control during the second half.

Even if our dreams turn nightmarish, we Americans still enjoy a good success story. We admire the discipline and fortitude it takes to become financially successful. Whether we want to admit it or not, we wish we had the qualities it takes to be financially independent. That's just being human. No matter how you define it, financial freedom is something we all want. We want it because we hate the thought of being dependent on others. While money doesn't buy happiness, we can all agree that we're sure happy to have it.

Over the years, I've counseled and coached all types of folks, from th`e very wealthy – those who shouldn't ever worry about money – to the very poor – those who have no money about which to worry. Both groups have one thing in common: regardless of how much money they have, they're all human. Both groups will worry about money. That's because it's not about the money! It's about you and what you do with what you have. Those who truly understand this may not be financially independent, but in my book, they are financial heroes.

What is a financial hero?

A financial hero is one who first admits they're human. They admit that they don't know it all, yet they accept responsibility to give it their all. They take life's journey seriously, they just don't take themselves too seriously. Their money is a means to an end, rather than an end to a means. A financial hero has a clear purpose in life because their destination is crystal clear. An informal study that I made of financial heroes reveals them to be very humble, content with what they have and not overly worried about the future. By their own definition, financial success is not measured by points on a scoreboard (how much money happens to be stockpiled away somewhere). Rather, they measure financial success by their life's journey and the positive impact it has had on others along the way. A financial hero is content with life and thankful for what they have.

Step Five: Admit You're Human

Sounds kind of boring, doesn't it? That's because it is not the world's view of success. The world's view is, "Get as much as you can, whenever you can." The world says that success is based on how much you make and how much you keep. The world is not overly impressed these days with humble people searching for contentment. If you don't believe me, just take a peek at prime time TV, and see how many shows promote serving "self" over serving others.

The world's definition of a financial hero is fuzzy because the world is human too. The only thing the world has to compare to is itself. Looking out for number one is number one. So we're taught the ways of the world through the human eyes of the world. Everything we know and do is based on someone else's experience of what we should be doing. We take other people's word for it because we are afraid to walk in another direction, even if that direction looks and feels safe to us. Because we're human, we follow the herd more times than not. We drink our water downstream from the rest of the herd and wonder why it tastes funny. We may occasionally worry that it's not safe, but hey, if it's good for them, its gotta be good for us, right?

Today's modern-day American is so busy accumulating material things that we have lost sight of why we work and what we're doing with our hard-earned money. We're more worried about planning to send our kids to expensive private universities than we are about taking care of them right now and instilling in them the values they need to get by in life. (Special note to parents and grandparents: speaking of financial heroes, your view of a financial hero will become your kids' and grandkids' view as well.)

Back in Granddad's day, it was a big deal to be worth a million dollars. Today, there's a millionaire next door. Folks, we've got plenty of millionaires to look up to – what we need are more financial heroes – people who may not be worth a million dollars, but are worth their weight in gold. We need everyday folks with vision and passion that goes beyond money. Remember, your journey cannot be just about money. If it is, you'll be disappointed with where you end up. Don't get me wrong; millionaires can be financial heroes – it's just a little harder. You see, as you begin to stockpile more and more money, something strange can occur; you begin to think it's not enough. You get worried that somebody's going to take it, so you build bigger barns. You become afraid to spend and enjoy your money. You may even become less charitable. Of course we all know of millionaires and billionaires who are philanthropists. Still it's human nature to become greedy for more. Getting money begets more of it.

Not so with a financial hero. My definition of a financial hero is someone who knows and understands their weaknesses. Because of this, financial heroes become disciplined. They create habits to protect themselves from veering off course. They become passionate, savvy, innovative and ambitious in ways that we could never imagine. This passion motivates them in their daily walk. Perfection is their dream. This attitude creates happiness and contentment that money can't buy. And their walk reflects it. Even if you don't have a million dollars in your 401(k), you can be a financial hero. First, you just admit you're human!

The key to dealing with your humanness is to drive the wedge of contentment between your circumstances and the negative feelings such as envy or fear that are so often arise from those circumstances. Contentment is the feeling you get when you aren't worried, or envious of what others have. It's accepting what you have and being appreciative for it. And, yes, this even includes times of great difficulty. Contentment is not easy. It can't be had overnight. The world's a tough place, and it has lots of stuff to throw at you. Contentment must be learned. It must evolve over your lifetime. That's why The WorryFree Retirement Process was created…to give folks a chance to focus on what's important and to take action toward a WorryFree contented life.

The first step is to learn to use the wedge of contentment properly. You use it when you see your neighbors building bigger houses, going on more trips than you, sending their kids to private schools, driving the latest SUV and having what appear to be more glamorous jobs than yours. You learn to strike a good balance between understanding what money is, and what it's for. Money is not a god; it's just a commodity. It's something that the world defines as being worth a certain amount, enabling you to exchange it for something else. While money can certainly buy you more time; it can't guarantee you'll be happy with the results.

So as you set your sights on becoming a financial hero, look to the things of others that you truly admire, and think about whether or not they are really worthy of your admiration. Look at the quality of their lives, rather than the quantity of their stuff. See them as human, just like you. Realize that they've had to take the same road you have. Granted, some have had more opportunities, but that doesn't mean you can't walk in stride with them. It really is up to you. Begin by creating a disciplined life through regular habits. Create habits that support your vision. Then, stay the course. Slow and steady is your aim. Remember, the journey is just as important and enjoyable as the ultimate destination. Your journey must include joy and contentment and whatever money comes along to help purchase the things in your lifestyle that you need and want. You've got to dream before you can plan. Most people are not big dreamers. But that's okay; you can learn. And by the way, a Retirement Specialist will have the training to help you organize your thoughts so you can dream.

For years, I have hosted a TV show geared toward helping people with their money. Over that time, I've received thousands of calls and emails from people needing help with their finances. Most of them are worried about something. The majority of the inquiries are from people I've never met. They all have interesting stories to share. My office does its best to handle each question based on their personal situation. I don't believe in blanket statements to fix people's worries. It's usually not that simple. But one thing I've learned is that they are all human.

Several years ago, we got an email from a couple who said they would like to talk to me about their retirement. As always, we responded to them, "Well, of course." I didn't know these people from Adam, as they were from another city. When we met, I guessed them both to be about 50 years of age. That was interesting, given the fact that their email had mentioned they were already retired. I was anxious to find out how they had accomplished this goal at such a young age. Here, roughly, is how the conversation went (the names have been changed to protect their privacy, of course):

Step Five: Admit You're Human

Tony: *Hello, Mr. and Mrs. Jones. It's very nice to meet you. I want to thank you for watching the TV show and for your interest in our services.*

Couple: *You're welcome. We're excited to hear your thoughts on what we can do to improve our retirement.*

Tony: Great. *Now, first of all, may I ask your ages?*

Mr. Jones: *Sure, I'm 52, and the little woman is 50.*

Tony: *How in the h-e-double hockey sticks were you able to retire at such a young age?!?*

Couple (simultaneously): *We won the lottery!*

Tony (with a little bit of a snicker): *No really, how did you pull it off?*

Couple (again, simultaneously): *As we said, we won the lottery.*

Tony (less snicker at this point): *Oh! Tell me more.*

Mrs. Jones: *Some 14 years ago, we won the lottery, which at that time was $2.5 million. We had two options: we could either take a lump sum of $1.6 million, or we could take $125,000 a year for 20 years.*

Tony: *Sounds like a lot of money...what's the problem?*

Mr. Jones: *Well, we've got six more years left of $125,000.*

Tony: *I'm still not sure what the problem is. Let me make sure I got this straight. You've been receiving $125,000 for the last 14 years and, in six more years, those payments stop. Is that correct?*

Step Five: Admit You're Human

Mr. Jones: *That's correct. Six years from now, we won't have any money coming in.*

Tony: *What in the world have you been doing these last 14 years?*

Mrs. Jones: *Having fun! You see, we had basically blue collar jobs and didn't make a lot of money up til the point where we won the lottery. After winning the lottery, we quit our jobs and started enjoying $125,000 a year.*

Tony: *So, you basically are saying that you ratcheted up your lifestyle when you went from $40,000 a year to $125,000 a year?*

Mr. Jones: *That's right. And don't get us wrong, we have really enjoyed the money. We've been able to buy a bigger house, do lots of things with the kids and just overall had a really good time. The problem is, we don't want to go back to work. And we realized that* *we've got to save all this money in the next six years.*

Tony: *So, you're expecting me to show you how to save enough money over the next six years so you'll never have to go back to work?*

Couple (simultaneously): *Well, basically.*

Tony: *Why is it you think you didn't save any money during the last 14 years?*

Mrs. Jones: *Well, we never understood how much taxes and inflation would eat away at this. I mean, let's face it, fourteen years ago, the thought of knowing we had $125,000 a year coming in every year was... well, that was more money than we could ever imagine. We didn't realize how quickly time would go by and we certainly didn't realize how easy it would be to spend this much money. We'd never had this much money before.*

Step Five: Admit You're Human

Tony: *I see, said the blind man. You know, this is no different than my clients who forget how quickly time goes by and don't save any money either. So, I guess I can understand how this might have happened. But there's nothing I can do to promise you, at your young age, that we can put money away to make sure you never have to go back to work. In fact, as I see it, you're probably going to have to go back to work.*

Couple (simultaneously, with a dazed and confused look on their faces): *Go back to work? Thank you very much...we'll get a second opinion...*

Now before you become too judgmental of our lottery winners, keep in mind that they're human. Ask yourself this question: "If I were that couple, would I have behaved the same way? Knowing I would receive $125,000 a year for the next 20 years, would I choose to enjoy the money, or sock it away like a squirrel? Would I quit my job?"

If you're honest with yourself, the answer is, "Who knows?"

Think back to your first full-time job. Remember your starting salary? I do. My first job paid $11,000 the first year. How much did you make? Probably wasn't much. So now, compare the salary of your first job to what you're bringing home now. Chances are, its a whole lot more today, than it was yesterday. Maybe it's more than you ever imagined making in your entire life. The question is: where did it all go? How much of that increase in salary do you have left?

Now ask yourself, "What would a financial hero do with all that money?" I believe, first and foremost, a financial hero would not change a great deal about their lifestyle. A financial hero would take that money and begin investing it in a safe place, realizing that inflation, taxes and the "lifestyle inflation" phenomenon (you know, those gadgets and gizmos) will take a toll on the money. But like I said, we're all human. Can you be so sure you would become a financial hero with such a windfall of cash?

It only takes one negative behavior or habit to affect the rest of your life. Receiving a windfall of $2.5 million will test anyone's character! It's a real test of one's discipline to use it in a manner that won't create more worry. It will challenge your original vision of the future. A huge lump sum payment like this one can actually be a financial tsunami – sweeping you off your feet as you look back one day trying to figure out what hit you. That brings us back to the entire philosophy of Perfecting Your Walk; staying the course, no matter what.

The purpose of Perfecting Your Walk is to create in you that desire for perfection, knowing all the while that perfection is not possible in this lifetime. Does this mean your quest is futile? Not at all. The "desire" for perfection is the perfection. That desire to see the destination creates in us a desire for discipline, for good habits. These habits keep us on the straight and narrow path regardless of whether we win the lottery, make seven figures, or just plod along on our regular salary.

The chances of winning the lottery are outrageously small, but people buy tickets every day. They buy them because there is something they hope for that only money can buy. We all buy "lottery tickets" every day. We buy them when we invest in things we don't understand. We buy them when we work longer hours for more income, not knowing if that extra money will really improve our lives or make us happy. We buy them when we try to spend money we don't have on things we don't need. We think money will solve our problems. But it won't. Remember, it's not about the money. It's about the discipline to create and enjoy it, all the while knowing it's really not the key to contentment. Chasing after money for money's sake will only create worry.

Creating a WorryFree Retirement™ begins with the clear vision we've spoken of in this book, and then setting up a plan of discipline around it. Americans have lost sight of discipline because they've lost sight of what it is they really want out of life. We'll eat fast food and gain forty pounds because we don't see any reason not to. We don't exercise because we think our spouses don't really need us and look at us the way they used to. We're so caught up in the world's picture of today that we've forgotten our own picture of tomorrow.

Step Five: Admit You're Human

When it comes to retirement, I believe that even if you make less money at a job you love, it'll be worth it down the road. This is because having a job that you enjoy is a part of Perfecting Your Walk. When you work at a job you love, you'll think less about retiring. You'll enjoy getting up every morning and be more content as a result. Now, that's my vision of a financial hero.

So if you're still worried about today's outdated notion of retirement, just forget it. Start today by focusing on your strengths and weaknesses. Just admit you're human. If you're not sure what you will do when you retire, maybe you need to plan on working longer at something you really enjoy. And if you don't enjoy doing what you're doing now, either go find something else to do or begin training yourself in an area that fits more with who you are and your vision for the future. And for you married couples out there, when you talk about retirement with one another, begin looking at your personal strengths and weaknesses. By doing so, you can head off a lot of problems down the road in your marriage. As a couple, you each are uniquely gifted with certain things the other spouse doesn't have. That's the beauty of marriage. Use your differences and unite them into a very secure marriage. A strong marriage will get you worrying less about your money in a hurry. You'll have more confidence when the two of you are on the same page. I recently met with a married couple in their late '50s. They told me they met in high school. They agreed that from day one, they were meant to be married. In high school, they even mapped out their financial goals for the future. I had never heard of such a thing. Anyway, after meeting with this couple for over an hour, the wife made a startling comment. She said that for first time in over 40 years, they had been arguing over money. Actually, it was about him retiring early. The wife said that up until now, everything was fine. But now, with him talking about calling it quits, she became worried that one day, they might run out of money. He thought they would be fine. She didn't. He had confidence and experience managing their stock portfolio. She was worried that she wouldn't know what to do with the portfolio if he died before she did.

The bottom line: Most women want and need more of a sense of security than do most men. Maybe it's cultural, maybe it's in our hard-wiring, or maybe it's a combination of both. My advice: remember, you're both human. So appreciate each other, all the while respecting your differences. Learn to meet each other half way when it comes to conflict over financial decisions. Communicate regularly with one another. Your marriage should be a wonderful partnership; don't let money and worry spoil it.

Okay, let's get back to the subject of discipline. Just how do you build discipline into your life? Where do all these wonderful habits come from? And here's another question you may have asked yourself (I sure have): Why do Americans spend billions of dollars each year on self-help books, yet, do very little work on improving their situation?

Let me answer that last question first, by identifying the culprit: Procrastination.

Procrastination is the world's ax of discouragement. It lets us see what could be, but tells us it's not possible. Procrastination whispers sweet nothings in our ear, telling us that by taking that first step, we could fail. It says, "Don't do it," when our heart says otherwise. Procrastination takes us to our greatest fears and worries, then magnifies them out of proportion. Because we're human, we procrastinate. Whether from fear, anxiety or just laziness, we all put things off for tomorrow that we know we need to do today.

Procrastination causes worry. It creates idleness and an attitude of feeling non-productive. Left unguarded, procrastination can even lead to depression. That's because as humans, we like to feel as though we are making progress in life. It's no fun going backwards, or going nowhere at all. If you want to create a WorryFree Retirement, you'll need to take action. That's what our next exercise will help you do. So if you're ready, let's take a little walk. Don't put it off...do it now!

Step Five: Admit You're Human

THE WORRYFREE RETIREMENT™ GUIDE: TWO-MINUTE WALK

I want you to imagine that today is your last day on earth. What would be your first action? Notice I didn't say "response"; I said "action." You just got this news, so what are you going to do about it? If you're a procrastinator, I guess you could just put it off one more day. Or, you could sit around the house for the rest of the day, thinking about what could have been. This unique tool is called The Last Day Planner™. It's purpose is to get you focused on today. So take a two-minute walk to see what motivates you to live and enjoy life more. As before, take your biggest worry and transfer it to the worksheet located at the end of the book.

Step 5   Admit You're Human

I'M WORRIED...

	Not Worried	Somewhat Worried	Very Worried
that we aren't taking enough time to travel.	1 2 3	4 5 6 7	8 9 10
that I'm not spending enough money on my family.	1 2 3	4 5 6 7	8 9 10
that I'm spending too much money on gadgets and gizmos.	1 2 3	4 5 6 7	8 9 10
that I don't have a special hobby or interest.	1 2 3	4 5 6 7	8 9 10
that I'm so uptight about money.	1 2 3	4 5 6 7	8 9 10
that nobody seems to care what happens when I die.	1 2 3	4 5 6 7	8 9 10
that I'm not having fun anymore.	1 2 3	4 5 6 7	8 9 10
that my life is boring and full of routines that don't seem to matter.	1 2 3	4 5 6 7	8 9 10
that others don't seem to worry about planning for retirement like I do.	1 2 3	4 5 6 7	8 9 10
that my spouse and I don't have the same interests.	1 2 3	4 5 6 7	8 9 10

MY BIGGEST WORRY IS...

_____

_____

(transfer to ActionPlanner on page 177)

Step Six

Take Responsibility

"Remember, when you point your finger at someone else, the other four are pointing at you." ~ Granddad

Quick, tell me: What are your goals in life? Are they written down? Could you spout them off the top of your head? Is there anyone else close to you who knows them? Is there anybody who holds you accountable to them?

Taking responsibility requires setting realistic goals. Without goals, there's no reason to accept responsibility. Think about it: if you never tell yourself what it is you wish to accomplish, nothing will ever be your fault. Financial failure, worry, lack of discipline in all areas of your life…it'll all just be someone else's problem.

If you do not have a mission in life and goals to support that mission, your life will ultimately seem meaningless. Your job, your spouse, your kids – nothing will have as much significance. That's because goals are evidence that you have a purpose, a vision. This is true about your life in general, and just about every aspect of your life – including your retirement. Without goals to support your retirement vision, your picture of the ideal retirement will be fuzzy at best. You are responsible for creating your vision for retirement. Only you can do this. Even if you don't have a clear vision of your future, you can create one. And you do not have to wander and stumble trying to find it.

In any game, sooner or later, you have to step up to the plate. If you don't go up there swinging, you're going to fail. When you step up to the plate and swing, either one of two things can happen; you swing and miss, or you swing and hit. Taking responsibility gives you the feeling that you're making the effort to improve your life in order to gain more control of it. When you take responsibility for things, your discipline and habits become more predictable and more challenging as well.

Step Six: Take Responsibility

My granddad's generation was one of the greatest generations our country has ever known. We can call them the World War II generation. These Americans endured one of the worst financial depressions this country has ever seen. They witnessed and fought in the biggest war this world may ever know.

At a time when our country was on the ropes, this bunch took responsibility for where they were and where they wanted to go. People from this generation have no problem telling us about the pressures of life back then. They took what the world had to offer them, dug in, and pulled themselves up by their bootstraps. They understood what it meant to accept risk, accept circumstances, and forge ahead against all odds.

By contrast, today it appears people are unwilling to take responsibility for anything – including their money and their retirement. They want to play the blame game for something that happened in the past or something they fear could happen in the future. They're unwilling to take responsibility for their lack of planning and goal setting. This is a big mistake, especially for those who want a WorryFree Retirement. If you refuse to take responsibility, you will worry.

Looking back on the '90s, I still feel somewhat guilty for having so much of my clients' money in the stock market. The go-go '90s was a period of time when everyone believed the market was a "new market." One "expert" back then predicted that the Dow could reach 30,000. Every advisor on TV, and even yours truly, believed that the gold rush of the stock market gains during the 90s would never stop. Then 2001 came.

For me, the realization that the market was over-inflated hit hard. As a money manager during that time, I could not continue to put people's money at risk. I was unwilling to take responsibility for a stock market that had no bearing or consistency to it. So, in the year 2002, I officially got out of the market and moved as many accounts as I could into safer territory.

But a short pencil is better than a long memory any day. What was so fresh and vivid on people's minds during the turn of the century is already forgotten. It was only a few years ago that many folks swore off the market, vowing that they would never again be so foolish as to invest all of their life savings into things they knew nothing about. But here we go again! Many of those same people are running back to the market. Now, they say, is a "good time" to get in because it has dropped so much. If that's your attitude, that's okay; just be sure to accept responsibility for the ups and downs of the market. A qualified Retirement Specialist can help you map out just how much you need at risk in the market – again, based on your vision and goals. It is possible to use the market as a starting point on the road to a safe and secure retirement. However, I strongly suggest you find a guide who can help you get there. Remember that this, too, is your responsibility.

Taking responsibility transforms you. In fact, as you set goals and plan your future, you'll gain more freedom in your life. Well-defined goals give you a sense of control. Goals provide the needed confidence to look outside the box. Goals strengthen your ability to accept change in order to deal with difficulties that lie ahead. Because we're human, and because this is the real world, things will not always work out as planned. But that doesn't mean you give up. Goals are important toward

Perfecting Your Walk in Retirement.

I haven't created the Responsibility Meter yet, but if I did, it would be based on age. The older you get, generally, the more responsible you become. So let's look at the following age groups to see what each person should consider taking responsibility for:

Ages 18-23: At this stage in life, you're just trying to find yourself. You've graduated high school and have no clue what you're doing. As of this writing, my oldest son falls here. After college, kids at this age hope to graduate with honors, at which time they imagine they will have recruiters from large corporations beating their door down with job offers, and then, of course, they will get the job of their dreams and live happily ever after. Of course, most of them are surprised to graduate with a four-year degree in hand that's simply a permission slip to spend four more years in college, earning a "professional" degree that actually gets them a job.

Step Six: Take Responsibility

Some young adults just skip the whole college deal and work full time, join the military or stay at home with Mom and Dad, contemplating the mystery of life.

The point is, this group is not in the real world just yet, but still in "the land of do as you please." This can be a very expensive time for parents. Whether their kids are home or away, the expenses still persist. When Granddad turned eighteen, he was run out of the house, never to be dependent on his parents again. Not so today. Due to the cost of living, many kids can't afford to live on their own. So parents, remember that the money you invest in your child's expenses will drain future retirement dollars. Yet you do have a responsibility to your child's future as well as to your own. And young people; you have a responsibility to do your best to take advantage of the opportunities being given you. If that's college, major in something that is in line with your vision and what you enjoy doing. Seek out others who have experience in your fields of interest who can share with you the realities of the field you are considering. Begin saving money… any amount will do! And don't procrastinate, because the longer you wait to save and invest money, the less control you'll have over it.

Ages 25-35: I remember this age well. Taking responsibility for retirement was the furthest thing from my mind. My wife and I were trying to buy our first home then. We were also trying to start a family. My main responsibility was finding a job and supporting my growing expenses. Luckily, my wife was a nurse (she didn't major in something stupid like I did). Her salary helped carry us those first few years. I never dreamed of putting money away for retirement. I didn't think we could afford it, not with all those techno-toys to buy (I remember when the VCR first came out – I just had to have one). I certainly did not understand the concept of the time value of money (the later you wait to save and invest, the less you have in the future). Being in the financial field, I quickly gained an understanding of money, but I was usually advising other people on their money and neglecting my own financial security. Don't laugh, it's a fact; most specialists in any field neglect to do what they preach to their clients. As an example, it's estimated that over 70% of attorneys die without wills. And we've all heard about the cobbler's children who have no shoes...

Step Six: Take Responsibility

So what if you are in this age range and don't take responsibility for putting money aside; what's the big deal? After all, you're still young. You have your whole life ahead of you. Well, that's my point exactly. Here's an example:

Bill and Jane have just married. They are both 25. If they would simply put away $2,000 per year in an account earning 5% interest (after taxes), the account would be worth $253,000 by the time they reach 65. However, if they wait till they are age 50, and put back the $2,000 each year, the account would be a whopping $45,000 when they reached age 65. Obviously, compound interest and the time value of money require time! Take responsibility and understand that time will go by very quickly. The old axiom really is true – time is money.

Another point of responsibility for this age group is to simply set aside "enough" money for retirement. Enough is never enough, but a good rule for saving is to put aside at least 15% of your gross income. For instance, if your income is $30,000, you should be putting away $4,500 a year. Don't worry about "where" to put this money, just put it away. Remember, you're trying to become disciplined by building good habits. At this point you're simply trying to take responsibility for setting money aside.

The 15% rule of thumb protects you from the effects of inflation. As your income increases, so will your savings. In other words, if your income grows to $50,000, you'll be saving $7,500 (15% of $50,000) instead of $4,500. I know this sounds overly simple, but it works. If you're serious about pursuing goals and dreams for the future, you'll just need to do it. Do this for the rest of your life and you'll never run out of money.

Ages 35-45: Currently I'm at the tail end of this group. Today, this group looks like a shopping spree gone mad. As noted earlier, we are way too busy spending money we don't have, to buy things we don't need, just to impress people we really don't like anyway. Although they're getting a little older, this group is still in the "first half." People in this age group are just now getting a feel for the flow of the game. They've scored some points, had some personal victories and are gaining confidence; they are caught up in the game. Many folks in this age range have two or three kids. Their kids are usually very active in sports and other personal endeavors. The family might be financially committed to spending money on sports, school, businesses, music lessons – you name it, they and their kids are in it. And all of these activities cost money.

This group is also technology-rich but financially poor. They own the latest cell phone technology, numerous televisions, PlayStations, flat screen TVs, Walkmans, DVDs, computers, iPods and the like, but very little cash. Look over your own list. Think about all the stuff you have in your home. Ask yourself, "How much of this stuff do I really need?" More importantly, how much is it costing you in lost opportunity cost for your retirement?

Eventually, all this stuff will be worthless. It will be of no value. This is called depreciation. Depreciation simply means that the things you buy will go down in value each year. And this is a huge hit to your finances. The cost of goods and services goes up each year, while the value of our stuff goes down. If you're into technology, this will really hit you hard. I'm still hanging onto my old 286 computer, which in 1989 was slower than smoke, yet cost me over $3,000. Anybody want to buy that thing?

Ages 45-65: Most of this age group is considered to be at half time or already starting the second half. They're in the locker room or have just come out of the locker room. In the real world, they have friends and relatives who have passed on. Some of them have experienced financial bankruptcy; some of them have created lots of wealth in real estate, stocks, or in their businesses. Many of them have had kids who have already died. Some of them have kids who are on drugs. Many of them have kids who are doing very well and are independent. Some in this age group are taking care of their aging parents, or they have already lost one or both parents.

This is the point in life where you really understand what the world's all about. You finally admit, perhaps for the first time, that time has passed quickly and the clock is ticking. This is the time of life which allows for deeper thought about your game plan. It's the point in time where there's no turning back, and you realize that responsibility is upon you. If you don't seize the moment during this period of time, a safe and secure retirement could be impossible for you. This isn't alarmist thinking or pessimism...it's called wisdom.

If you're still in half time, you are still in the "accumulation" stage. Everyone's telling you to sock away as much as you can. By now, with the kids out of the household – or so you hope – you have more time to do what you want to do, and hopefully some money to do it with. You're traveling more. You know your tastes in food, music and entertainment. You have a pretty good feel for what retirement might look like. On the down side, there is the inevitable physical decline. You may find yourself taking more naps. And you begin to start worrying about bodily functions that may not have been such a concern when you were younger. If you're smart you'll consider all of these things a wake-up call. This age is the perfect time to really clarify your vision for the future and take responsibility. By now, you understand the importance of putting money away, and you know a thing or two about the time value of money. If you haven't done so already, this is a perfect time to take responsibility and establish your game plan. It's not too late, believe me.

It's pretty obvious why people in this age group should worry about retirement. By now they realize the clock is ticking. They're at or near the second half. They can't go back and repeat the first half, much as they might like to. They realize how experienced their "opponent" is. They know that it will be difficult to win the game. Roller coaster stock markets, increasing taxes, inflation, health scares, kids needing financial help, all add up to more worry. People in this group often don't know when to invest and when not to invest. They pool their money and put it on the sidelines, only to get 2% interest. Their coach (financial advisor) really doesn't seem to be helping matters as the opponent starts catching up. They watch the scoreboard and get nervous. They begin listening to the crowd noise and begin shooting air balls (missing the basket entirely). And their coach isn't helping them. So they begin to lose hope and feel defeated. After some time, they won't even shoot the ball (spend money) for fear that the opponent will take it away.

This is no way to wind down life! But it really does not have to be that way. You and your Retirement Specialist can take control,

Step Six: Take Responsibility

if you take responsibility. Remember, taking responsibility is all about time, and time is precious. Without it, you cannot accomplish the dreams that you have for the future. Time is your most important asset.

Ages 65+: What can I say? If you fall into this age range, you are probably well into the second half. This is the "distribution" phase – the time in your life when you should be spending and enjoying your money, not hoarding it up for others to enjoy when you die. In the second half of the financial game, your opponent (everyone who is after your money) is breathing down your neck. The scoreboard may show that you are ahead, but you're starting to feel the pressure. The other team's gaining on you and you know it. Fear and uncertainty fill your mind. Knowing you have to keep playing until the final horn sounds gives little hope. It's too late to go to the bench for a breather, and there will be no more halftime chats in the locker room. You may even feel it's too late to get another coach.

But it is not too late – not yet. However, in order to create a WorryFree Retirement at this stage, you will need to act quickly. Time is running out. You may even have to make drastic changes like moving money out of high-risk funds and into safer investments and instruments. While being debt free always made sense for Granddad, you may have to resort to using your home's equity for distribution planning. You have some time outs left – so use them. Get with your coach and look at your current strategy. Begin with a vision, a dream, of what you want and how you will use and enjoy what's left. If your current coach can't help you, fire him and get another one. Locate a Retirement Specialist who sees the entire floor, one who can react quickly and keep your vision as safe as possible. There is so much to consider during the second half. How much will health care cost? Will I have to go into a nursing home or assisted living facility? Should I be giving money to my kids, grandkids and/or charity? How much money should I invest in the stock market? Are bonds the right choice? Should I annuitize any money and take a guaranteed income for the rest of my life? Should I spend or defer my IRA? Should I invest the time and money in Living Trusts? These are huge decisions that require time with someone who can formulate them into your own game plan.

In my world, I always trust in hope. Having hope in something breeds responsibility. Hope gives you courage to seek different ways of doing things. Hope reinforces the truth. Hope gives you focus, and focus gives you confidence to stay on track. Your walk must be guided by hope or you will surely veer off course. Without hope, you will worry. You can be certain that your opponent will not give you hope. It's up to you to establish your own vision for the future and learn the rules of the game.

Finally, if you are under the age of 65 and feeling pressure to retire at age 62 or 65 like Granddad's generation did, you may need to think again. In light of the circumstances discussed in this book, you may realize that working longer isn't such a bad idea after all. You just need to find something you enjoy doing. Working hard at something you enjoy is the world's most honorable profession. It's one of the wonderful characteristics of a financial hero. Here's my take on life. As long as I'm enjoying what I'm doing and God gives me the strength to do it, I plan on working (in some capacity) forever. Why would I ever stop?

The second half of life should be a time in our life when wisdom and experience is considered superior by the rest of the world. We have rid ourselves of many false notions and opinions and are much savvier about the way the world works. Our society should cherish the wisdom of our elders. Unfortunately, our youth-oriented culture has developed a disrespect for age, and old age is looked upon by many as a disease. Our elderly have become almost a class of untouchables, and this is a shame. On the other hand, our elders should cherish the responsibility that goes along with possessing their hard-earned wisdom. Yet many older people become overly self-absorbed and isolated, and at some point many stop growing and reaching out to the world. Maybe if older people and the rest of the world would agree to meet each other halfway, we could all benefit. Let's face it, wisdom only comes through time, and this age group has experienced lots of both.

For those of you are under 65, as you consider the financial struggles seniors are having today, don't think for a minute that your financial situation will be any better. Uncertainty over Social Security, fewer pensions provided by employers, potential stock market losses, housing bubbles – all of these factors seriously affect your retirement. So what are you going to do about it now?

If you're in the first half or at halftime, here's my suggestion: invest in yourself. Over the past ten years, I have literally spent hundreds of thousands of dollars on my vision, "to help more and more people, worry less and less about money." That's why I think God put me here. While I enjoy money, to me, it's not about the money. Lots of "stuff" doesn't do much for me. I got over my "stuff obsession" not too long after I got that first VCR. You see, I've come to realize that to spend too much money on material things takes away from my vision and mission in life. I'd rather spend most of my money on intellectual ideas for training so I can better perform my duties for the clients whom I serve. I work with many financial institutions (I place my clients' money with them) but I don't work for any of them (I'm not employed by any, so they can't tell me where to put my clients' money). With the majority of my income coming from the clients I serve, I feel it is my responsibility to take that money and invest it back in myself for the purpose of continuing to grow in knowledge so I can better the community and world in which I live. It's my responsibility to do that, and that's my vision for the future. And yes, it's very exciting and rewarding to think about what I will be doing to help people twenty, thirty or even fifty years from now.

How about you? What will you be doing fifty years from now?

Step Six: Take Responsibility

THE WORRYFREE RETIREMENT™ GUIDE: TWO-MINUTE WALK

Whether you just started college, are beginning the first half of life, sitting in the locker room at halftime, or watching the clock wind down during the second half of life; there's still time on the clock. It just takes a personal commitment to be responsible for creating that vision of what retirement will look like for you. Your vision will create hope. But you must set up a game plan for retirement. It's the responsible thing to do. This should be your number one priority. The game plan must compete successfully against your opponent. To help you, I have created something called the Responsibility Prioritizer. This two-minute walk will help you gain more insight into what you need to do today to take more responsibility.

Step 6 Take Responsibility

I'M WORRIED...	Not Worried	Somewhat Worried	Very Worried
that I'm not educated as to all of the options available to me.	1 2 3	4 5 6 7	8 9 10
that I'm not taking my finances serious enough.`	1 2 3	4 5 6 7	8 9 10
because I don't understand taxes and how they impact my retirement.	1 2 3	4 5 6 7	8 9 10
because I'm working harder, and making less money.	1 2 3	4 5 6 7	8 9 10
that I won't be able to provide for my family.	1 2 3	4 5 6 7	8 9 10
that I feel stupid when I speak with financial advisors.	1 2 3	4 5 6 7	8 9 10
that I haven't taken time to create my own personal game plan.	1 2 3	4 5 6 7	8 9 10
that my money is at risk and out of my control.	1 2 3	4 5 6 7	8 9 10
that I don't have adequate insurance protection.	1 2 3	4 5 6 7	8 9 10
that I don't have a trusted advisor.	1 2 3	4 5 6 7	8 9 10

MY BIGGEST WORRY IS...

_____

_____

(transfer to ActionPlanner on page 177)

Step Seven

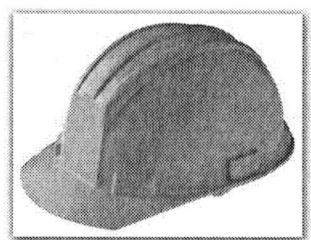

Work Hard
(But Just Slow Down)

"There's a difference between 'hard work' and 'working hard'. One requires lot's of energy; the other requires lot's of passion." ~ Tony Walker

The American way of life is being blamed for a lot of the world's woes. The industrialized nature of our country has created great opportunities and problems throughout the world. With technology, other countries can now "link" into our way of life with the click of a mouse. More and more work is being outsourced overseas. Certainly, much of the world is a better place because of Americans' ingenuity and hard work. So why do some people around the world resent Americans?

I guess for the rest of the world, especially those who live in poverty, we probably are a confusing bunch. They would be even more confused – perhaps even alarmed – to hear how much we worry and stew over money. And as for retirement – well, much of the world's population doesn't even relate to retirement. Where they come from, there is no such notion.

In America, we worry over the price of gasoline, while in other parts of the world, they worry where their next meal will be coming from. We get outraged that we don't have HDTV, they are thankful that they don't have HIV (although, sadly, many do). We willingly pay hundreds of dollars a year for bottled water that tastes just like tap water; they have little of either.

I can understand how the rest of the world feels about us. What the world forgets, though, is that Americans are very hardworking and industrious. Our capitalistic mentality fosters a people that live by a positive, can-do attitude. It doesn't hurt that our country is blessed with great resources. Arguably, while Americans may be less willing to take personal responsibility (look at the number of lawsuits today versus Granddad's day),

Step Seven: Work Hard (But Just Slow Down)

we are still a people that believes "the buck stops here." We're highly motivated. Success is rewarded – failure is not. And, assuming the government doesn't regulate and tax us to death, many successful people will follow in this tradition. The United States has boundless opportunities. This is good.

Since we're all human, I think it's safe to say that everyone from Russia to Africa possesses the same desires and goals. I believe that everyone is born for a reason. We arrive in this world wanting to be fulfilled, to provide for our families and to have purpose in our lives. I believe this purpose is achieved through a man or woman's vocation – their calling in life, if you will. In other words, we are wired for work.

So if we're wired for work, why are we so preoccupied with retirement? If hard work creates success and security, why would we ever plan to stop working at some predetermined age? It's a good thing our forefathers had a purpose, or we would really be up a creek. Can you imagine George Washington breaking the news to his Continental Army that instead of finishing off the British, he'd be retiring to a scenic cabin in the woods of Kentucky?

Here's the truth: hard work builds character, character fuels passion and passion confirms hope. Boil all of these ingredients down and you've got contentment. Not worry, contentment – the kind of contentment a financial hero wakes up with each and every day. Because remember, it's not about the money, it's about working hard and enjoying what you have.

Still, there has to be a balance. The WorryFree Retirement™ Process includes working harder, but slowing down. It doesn't mean 60-hour work weeks, it simply means that we work when we need to, not because we have to. We work because that is our calling in life. And the fruits of our labor are a day's wages so we can enjoy our time here on this earth. Perfecting Your Walk strikes a new balance. It's certainly about working hard, but it's also about slowing down to enjoy the journey – knowing that the journey could end when we least expect it. There are no guarantees that the road you are on will always be easy. In fact, it's pretty certain that the road will be immensely difficult at times. If you live long enough, you

Step Seven: Work Hard (But Just Slow Down)

will encounter obstacles unforeseen by any man. But that's just part of the journey.

Hard work doesn't mean mad dashes to nowhere. The real question for retirement is: "Should we work harder, or slow down and work longer?" I see many folks working hard and making lots of money, but they have little joy to show for it. They are in serious danger of burning out. When that happens, they lose interest in their jobs, their family, their marriage, their goals, their health, their bodies, and worse yet, their faith. They may have money, but they may also feel discontent. Their gadgets and gizmos no longer interest them. The new toys just don't bring the joy they used to. In general, they simply lose hope. In basketball, no team can fast break for every minute of each half. And neither can you. If you do, eventually, you'll run out of gas. There's no victory in that game plan.

That's why Perfecting Your Walk is about a slow and steady pace. It's not trying to be like the Titanic, speeding across the ocean thinking all is well. You have to be on the lookout for icebergs. You must stay at the helm and keep a watchful eye out. That is the responsible thing to do. It's why you were created in the first place. Remember, we are talking about your life's work, and the only way to do justice to your life and your work is to just slow down.

Regardless of how much money you make, your current vocation should have a mission statement. Mine is: *"I want to help more and more people worry less and less about their money."*

You can create your own personal mission statement as well, and I hope this book is giving you the information and tools to do that. Your mission statement must come from your vision of where you want to be in life. A personal mission statement sums up who you are, and what you wish to accomplish with your life. It takes discipline and a sincere desire to practice healthy habits. A mission statement should include your passion, what it is you love doing for yourself, and others. You should be able to share it in twenty seconds or less. I call this my elevator speech. A mission statement is a reflection of what's most important to you and sharing it with others. If you don't have a mission statement, don't worry, this just means you need to

Step Seven: Work Hard (But Just Slow Down)

focus on it and write it down.

Your work, whether you're out of the work force or a stay-at-home parent, should have purpose and meaning. Even if you are employed and feel that the job you have now is not an ideal reflection of your purpose in life, you can still create a mission statement. It is my hope that you will be inspired to find a career that is more in keeping with who you are. If, however, it's a situation you can't change, take responsibility for where you are now and develop your own mission statement for work, based on your vision for retirement. It will give you hope, I can assure you. Also remember that even though work is an important part of who we are, we are much more than the work we do.

No matter how much you love what you do, there's another good reason to be realistic about all of this hard work, and to learn to pace yourself. As you grow older, you will have to slow down! This is a physical issue for all of us. At my age, I've noticed that it's harder for me to work longer hours. I just physically can't do it. That's why you must take time to exercise and watch your diet. Believe me, as you get older, you'll need all the extra energy you can muster.

So how do you begin to work hard and slow down? Build into your life daily habits that help you keep an even pace. Even if you're in the first half of the game, be careful not to work long hours – no matter how much you love your work or want to "get ahead." Not only will you get burned out, you'll also miss many of life's simple pleasures – like watching your kids grow up along the way. It's hard to enjoy things when you are running by them. Work hard, but keep an even pace. Stay on the trail to your destination. Keep focused on your future goals. Work at a pace that could possibly be maintained for the rest of your life.

Here's a real-life example of working hard, but just slowing down. I have a client who works as a nurse for a physician. This physician is 79 years old. My client says her boss is going strong and is still very sharp. And his body is going strong as well; evidenced by the number of patients he sees every day. She says he has a great attitude towards life. He loves his work. He also tries to take care of himself. My client says one of his rituals is to have a peanut butter and jelly sandwich everyday for lunch. (Well, there just went the peanut butter stocks shooting through the roof, right?) My client says her boss is a pleasure to work with and continues to be highly motivated helping people through his medical skills.

Now, that's the kind of thing I'd like to be doing at age 79. Not necessarily seeing patients and eating peanut butter and jelly sandwiches at lunch, but I would like to be helping people in some capacity and actually getting paid for it. What a life!

Many baby boomers today are kidding themselves. As we've discussed, they have no clue what retirement is going to look like for them. They've been so busy raising their families, earning money and buying lots of "stuff" that they've never stopped to take a realistic snapshot of the future. Based on what I'm seeing, the vast majority of baby boomers will have to work, in some form or fashion, well past age 65. My advice, once again, is to find something you love doing, work hard at it, and have fun while you're doing it.

If you retire "too soon," you run the risk of forcing yourself into burnout. Here's how.

Setting unrealistic early retirement goals forces you to work harder and possibly risk more money. When I meet with couples contemplating early retirement, I usually uncover that one spouse is not in favor of the early retirement plan, but is afraid to challenge it because they don't know where to start. It takes a trained Retirement Specialist to pull it all together and determine if such a plan is possible or not. Certainly, there's nothing wrong with wanting to slow down at a young age, or even changing vocations, but be careful of setting a goal of trying to completely retire at some designated age in the future. There are too many variables out there that you can't control. And if you focus too strongly on the "destination," you may find yourself unable to enjoy the journey. Worse, once you get "there," you may discover that, as Gertrude Stein once said, "there *is* no there." In other words, you're possibly setting yourself up for a big disappointment, at best.

Step Seven: Work Hard (But Just Slow Down)

If you're still not convinced of the need for balance between work and the rest of life, let me illustrate my point with a brief story about twin brothers. While the characters in the story are make-believe, their stories are based on real-life examples that I have seen. Maybe you will see some resemblance to yourself in one of them.

Jim and John were born identical twins. Growing up, they were very similar. They looked exactly alike, they played ball together, and they did well in elementary and junior high school. As they approached high school, however, differences between the two began emerging. Jim developed a desire to make more and more money when he grew older. His idea of life was to make as much as he could, acquire a lot of toys and live off the land, so to speak. At a young age, Jim made it his goal to enter the medical field. He'd observed the lifestyles of the doctors around town, and decided this would be the path to take. After high school, Jim completed a four-year college degree in only three years. He went on to medical school as planned. Jim had to borrow several hundred thousand dollars to get through medical school. Slaving away, he eventually graduated and became a doctor. Putting in upwards of 70 hours per week, working hard and making lots of money, Jim's goal was to quit work at age 55 and go live on a beach somewhere. Over time, Jim realized his goal by accumulating boat loads of money, just as he had envisioned.

Brother John, on the other hand, enjoyed his high school years very much. He didn't really have any long-term goals about what he would do for a living. He played sports and got along with everybody. He graduated and decided to pursue a four-year degree in management at a local university. During that time, John discovered that he was very good with people. He enjoyed seeing other people doing well. John had a team spirit and attitude about everything he did. He went to college too, but he only spent about $3,000 each year on his four-year degree (remember this was years ago, when college wasn't so expensive). After four years, John graduated and immediately got a job making $25,000 a year. Keep in mind that while John was out in the work force making money, rather than borrowing money for medical school, Jim was still in medical school, spending hundreds of thousands of dollars trying to prepare for his lifelong dream to become a doctor. John's yearly salary of $25,000 increased between 6%-10% each year, and he quickly rose up the corporate ladder. He was doing a great job in management and developed lots of skills that people wanted. John averaged working between 40-50 hours a week, five days a week. He spent a lot of time with family, attended church on a regular basis and took time to coach his kids' sports teams. John loved working with people. It wasn't unusual to see him taking extra time to help people solve problems in their personal lives. John had a unique gift for understanding how to make complex things simple. He was always on the lookout for ways to improve people's lives. A wonderful manager, he was valued by the employers he worked for over the years.

Over that period, John took time to really map out his vision for the future. He realized from working with people that everyone's situation was different and that he would have to take responsibility for what he wanted for himself and his family. He began to support various organizations around town, so that his community could be improved. He figured that if he was going to live there for the rest of his life, he wanted to make it the best place possible.

John continued taking management courses on the side to improve his skills. His life was in balance; faith first, wife second, family third, and work fourth. He was mindful of time. His job required him to understand time management. He learned to apply the same time management skills to his life. He always tried to keep other people in the forefront of his mind.

Now, let's fast-forward. Jim and John are both age 65 and retired. They have met their life goals and fulfilled their dreams. Jim wanted to live in the Bahamas at age 55, and he was able to accomplish that. John wanted to be helping others through his work at age 55, and he did that as well. Those were their dreams financially. So let's take a look at where their lives are at this point, ten years later.

At age 65, John is still married to his high school sweetheart and doing consulting work for corporations on the side. Jim (the doctor) is now on his third wife, (soon to be his third ex-wife).

Step Seven: Work Hard (But Just Slow Down)

John spends a great deal of time with his kids and grandkids; Dr. Jim barely knows his. John's health is great; Jim just had triple bypass surgery and is taking multiple prescription medications because of poor health.

Jim still lives in the Bahamas (by himself) contemplating the meaning of life. Meanwhile, John is back home enjoying his family, work and continuing to improve his community.

John has about $500,000 in his retirement account. He has plenty of life insurance to protect his family and has created an exit strategy to use and enjoy every penny in his retirement account. He is still disciplined and continues to watch his spending. He understands the value of real estate and other investment opportunities and has a few things going there as well. John takes time to do lots of traveling with his wife and loves visiting with his kids and grandkids around the country. In fact, John's kids and grandkids still come to visit him on a regular basis. John is still excited about helping others and feels blessed with what God has provided him. He is thankful and continues to look out for the needs of others.

Brother Jim is burned out and bored. Living in the Bahamas by himself, his third wife just filed for divorce. It looks like Jim will be losing more of his assets because of it. Now, while Jim still has a million dollars in his retirement account, he's starting to get nervous about whether that money will last. Two years ago, his account was worth $2 million, but due to stock market problems and some risky investments, it was cut in half. Jim's retirement is anything but worry-free. While Jim has more money than 99% of the people in the world, he has no passion or joy for anything. He certainly is not content. He is riddled with guilt about his choices in life, even about whom to leave his money to.

Which twin does your life most resemble? Which one of them would you enjoy hanging out with? Which one would you enjoy working for? Our next two-minute walk will help you gain a new perspective on work and what it means to you.

Step Seven: Work Hard
(But Just Slow Down)

THE WORRYFREE RETIREMENT™ GUIDE: TWO-MINUTE WALK

Nothing in life comes easy. Only through hard work and sacrifice will you truly enjoy the fruits of your labor. However, your life must strike a balance. There must be a pace that sustains your walk for the rest of your life. In order to help you, we're going to take a two-minute walk down a path called the Infinite Career Builder. This walk will help you think about your retirement and what you would really like to be doing and what you could possibly do for the rest of your life.

Step 7 Work Hard (But Just Slow Down)

I'M WORRIED...

	Not Worried	Somewhat Worried	Very Worried
that I don't enjoy work anymore.	1 2 3	4 5 6 7	8 9 10
that I don't seem to have a passion for anything.	1 2 3	4 5 6 7	8 9 10
that I'll have to work for the rest of my life.	1 2 3	4 5 6 7	8 9 10
that my work involves being around people that I don't like.	1 2 3	4 5 6 7	8 9 10
that my work is too lonely.	1 2 3	4 5 6 7	8 9 10
that I don't have a chance to be creative.	1 2 3	4 5 6 7	8 9 10
that my job is too stressful.	1 2 3	4 5 6 7	8 9 10
that my work doesn't utilize my skills and gifts.	1 2 3	4 5 6 7	8 9 10
that my work takes too much time away from family.	1 2 3	4 5 6 7	8 9 10
that there is no future in what I'm doing.	1 2 3	4 5 6 7	8 9 10

MY BIGGEST WORRY IS...

_____

_____

(transfer to ActionPlanner on page 177)

Step Eight

Have Fun
(Just Be Sure To Bring Someone With You)

"There's a big difference between being entertained and having fun. One requires money – the other, imagination."
~ Tony Walker

I always enjoyed being around my granddad. He never seemed to take himself, and life, too seriously. He worked hard, took responsibility for his family, never worried what others thought of him and always was ready for a laugh. Unlike granddad, today, people appear way too serious.

For instance, I attend parent meetings at school. I'm around them at ball games. I watch them fret over the fact that their kid isn't "achieving" enough in school, or that he/she isn't getting enough playing time, etc. These, too, may be symptoms of taking life too seriously. Examples like these are more than just obsessions: they sometimes force us to place undue burdens on others. Even our children's activities can become an extension of ourselves. In everyday life, I see a lot of people coming and going. I see them doing things with their family. I even see them driving nice cars and living in big homes – but oddly enough, I don't see them having as much fun as they used to. Oh sure, we can all find something fun to do, but that usually costs hundreds, if not thousands, of dollars. A family of four can't go to a major league ball game for less than a couple of hundred dollars. Even spending the day at a local amusement park – and we're not talking Disney World, either – can put a serious dent in your wallet. Going to a first-run movie isn't cheap either, even if it's a matinee. Yet today, it's a whole lot easier just to go out and buy our fun rather than use our imagination and creativity to make our own fun. However, buying fun is expensive and is another cause for worry.

Step Eight: Have Fun

By now you may be protesting, "But, Tony, there's nothing to do any more that doesn't cost money. I mean, how are we supposed to have fun when all we do is run our kids all over God's country trying to get to the next ball game?" Listen, I hear you, and I understand. But believe me, there are ways to have fun for very little money. You just have to use your imagination, and a sense of humor doesn't hurt either.

My wife, Susan, and I have three children; Phillip, Lacey and Anthony. Anthony's the youngest. My wife refers to him as Tony number two, only worse. She blames me for his "unorthodox" sense of humor, which I'm actually quite proud of. I love to laugh, and so does Anthony. We have the same imagination. If we're out in public together, chances are, we're seeing something funny in somebody or something that no one else seems to notice. That's because everyone's taking life too seriously to see it.

When I'm in the mood, Anthony will talk me into playing a little game called "The Drive-Through Delusion." It's particularly fun when Anthony has a friend riding in the car with us. Here's how it works: We'll be driving around and decide on a soft drink or whatever. I'll pull into the nearest fast food restaurant (any fast food restaurant with a drive-through window will do). We immediately pull up to what I call the "Talking Sign." I roll down my car window, anxiously awaiting the garbled voice on the other end, who always asks, "May I take your order, please?"

The Drive-Through Delusion has now officially started.

I respond to the Talking Sign in one of my favorite voices. I have several cultural and ethnic variations – but my favorite voice has to be the "country bumpkin" voice. I perfected this years ago working as a lonely college kid on the weekend shift for a small town radio station. On Sundays, after all the preachers and gospel singers had done their thing, I was left all alone with my ten listeners (if that many) to do as I pleased. As long as I didn't get too crazy, I could try out all of my impersonations live, on the air, for the rest of the day. Thus, the "country bumpkin" voice of Ellwood P. Goldrush was born.

Step Eight: Have Fun

It just so happens that old Ellwood has developed a taste for fast food, but he takes his fast food quite seriously – and that's where the fun part comes in. After hearing the Talking Sign ask for my order, I usually respond to the question with a long drawn-out question of my own. "What comes on the num'er 5? How come the chicken sandwich don't have any special sauce on it, an' whar can I find out?" The questions can be quite a test for the Talking Sign. Today's Talking Signs, in case you haven't noticed, like to hear numbers, not questions. Depending on the Talking Sign's response, the order can take several minutes to complete. The country bumpkin voice just adds to the confusion. But they never catch on that it's not real; after all, this is the state of Kentucky, where the country bumpkin voice is accepted, tolerated, and in some small towns, quite appreciated.

With the conversation with the Talking Sign over, the Drive-Through Delusion isn't. The person on the other end of the sign hasn't yet seen the face behind the voice, and vice versa. As we pull around the corner to the first window to pay for our order, we meet face to face. The attendant usually has a somewhat anxious look as they wait to see the bumpkin behind the voice. Much to their surprise, around the corner comes an average looking, 45-year-old white Caucasian guy in a business-type vehicle. When I pull up to the window to pay, however, I can't say a word; otherwise, it would blow my cover. I simply hand them the money and smile. At this point, my son Anthony is having trouble containing himself. He usually looks out the passenger side window, trying not to laugh. If my wife happens to be with us, she looks out the window so no one will see her! For some reason (Anthony and I have never been able to figure out) Susan doesn't see the humor in all of this. The attendant at the first window hands me my change and says, "Thank you." Again, I can't use my country bumpkin voice at this point, or it would blow my cover. But we're still not done. We've got one more window to go to – the pick-up window.

By the time we get to the pick-up window, this person is laughing as they see what's going on. Again, since I don't want to blow my cover, I can't say anything to this person either. By this time, Anthony and I can't contain ourselves. The person at the pick-up window is usually laughing too. The Drive-

Step Eight: Have Fun

Through Delusion ends by me grabbing my order and driving off into the sunset. And for the small price of a few soft drinks or fast-food treats, I have brought laughter not only to my family (well, at least some members), but even to a couple of perfect strangers.

I'm confident everyone has a funny bone in their body. Some people just don't know where it's located. The key is to re-discover what makes you laugh. You may have to go back into childhood (hey, shrinks go back in childhood to discover problems, why not go back into childhood to see what made you laugh?). Think about the things you really enjoyed as a kid and what you had the most fun doing. If the thought of something years ago brings a smile to your face, you're on the right track. Laughter really is good for the soul. When you're laughing, you are smiling. And when you smile, you can't worry. It's physically impossible to look worried anyway, with a big smile plastered on your face. There's an old saying, "If you're happy, your face will tell you so."

Having fun is a big part of Perfecting Your Walk. If you aren't having fun, if there's no joy in what you are doing, what's the point? Hopefully, you're starting to realize that a WorryFree Retirement is not all about the money. It's about getting to a point in life where the journey is just as enjoyable as reaching the final destination. Joy and laughter set a path that makes life easier to bear. What you see as funny is strictly based on your personality and the things that bring joy to you. And it begins by not taking yourself, your job and even the people around you, quite so seriously.

What's the big reason that people aren't having fun anymore? I believe it is because they're leading other people's lives. Monkey see, monkey do. I'm reminded of lyrics from an old Janis Ian song, "Between the Lines": "We live beyond our means on other people's dreams, and that's succeeding..." As I discussed a while ago, too many people try to "buy" their fun. They follow the herd, waiting in line for hours to enjoy a 60-second thrill ride. And the world gets paid big money to entertain us. What a shame. Worse yet, since so many people don't have a clear vision for the future, they don't have any opportunity to laugh and have fun. They're too busy worrying about the future to have fun!

I've said it before and I'll say it again: When you create a vision for the future, you will build purpose in your life. And being less worried about the future allows you to see the joy of today. Your daily walk will be your focus. When you experience having fun, you'll walk more and run less. You will look more at what you are doing with your life, rather than wasting time watching others live theirs. Don't be fooled by the cover of your neighbor's "book" – by the way their lives look on the outside, and all the "stuff" they have. In my line of work, I get to see them without their cover – without their financial clothes on, if you will. I see the scars, the guilt, the worry, and even the lack of hope. I see the cover but I also see what's inside. Believe me, just because people have more today than Granddad ever imagined, that doesn't mean they know how to enjoy it. Granddad knew how to have fun with what he had; many of us don't.

Okay, so what's your definition of fun? A judge was once asked to define pornography, to which he responded: "I don't know how to define pornography, but I know it when I see it." Like our judge, I don't know how to define fun and joy, but I sure know it when I see it. You can create your own version of the Drive-Through Delusion; you just have to use your imagination. Take the time to see the world around you as just that – a world that should not be taken so seriously. This world, and the things in it, will soon pass. If you don't believe me, just go visit your neighborhood yard sale and look at all of the stuff being sold for pennies on the dollar. Most of these things probably seemed pretty cool to their owners when they were first purchased. But it's amazing how "I've just gotta have it!" can morph into, "What in blazes was I thinking?!?" Look at all of these cast-away toys as a metaphor. Don't take yourself so seriously, because nobody else is. What is such a worry today will soon be a distant memory anyway, so just enjoy today for what it is: another day.

"But Tony, you don't understand! My 401(k) is down 50%, I've got too much debt, I just lost my job, I'm spending more than I'm making, I'm on my second marriage and it's worse than the first one, and I don't see my kids any more. What's there to laugh about?"

Part of Perfecting Your Walk is to acknowledge that the world is not perfect, and neither are we. But just because the world is 'imperfect' doesn't mean we can't have fun while we're here. The fact is, the many problems and struggles we face are simply proof that the world is a tough place to do business. It's no cakewalk. Still, have you noticed that what worried you yesterday is often replaced by the worries of today? Again (thinking back on that yard sale), "this too shall pass." Time has a way of taking care of worries. Worrying, however, solves nothing. It certainly doesn't mean you'll stop worrying; quite the opposite is generally true. Worry by itself is a waste of time, having fun isn't.

I know it's not fun watching your 401(k) balances tumble 50%; it is fun to know that you still have something left to work with. We can't control the circumstances of life, but we sure can control our reactions to them. Worry is just a sign of how we react. Remember the WorryMeter we talked about in Step One? Our built-in WorryMeter tells us when we are taking ourselves too seriously. The purpose of the WorryMeter is to focus on the "big" worries and put a plan in place to do something about them. Moral to the story: If you're worried about something you can control, then take action and do something. If, on the other hand, you're worried about things you can't control, then keep reading.

After years of attempting to find the "magic bullet" of investments, I discovered something: there is no "magic bullet." There is no financial product out there that will keep you from worrying about your retirement. That's why I created The WorryFree Retirement™ Process. Until The WorryFree Retirement Process came along, there was no conversation taking place between consumers and their advisors which allowed the two of them to connect. Because the two parties had no common process, they continually focused on the wrong thing – trying to find that elusive "magic bullet" (the latest stock, the mutual fund with the best track record, the perfect annuity, term life insurance, paying off your home

Step Eight: Have Fun

early, maxing out your 401(k) plan). On the other hand, with a process built into the conversation, both consumer and advisor are working together as a team, rather than as potential adversaries (e.g., advisor picks the wrong stock and loses all of the client's money; client isn't having fun any more).

The WorryFree Retirement Process is about "how" to create a game plan for your future. While the products (the "where") are important to the process, they are not to be confused with the process itself. Think of it the way you would a car. The engine (the product) makes the car run so you can drive it. But an engine doesn't make the car any safer. The engine is only as good and safe as the driver (you and your advisor) and the components (process) that go into making the car drive. If the engine runs too fast (e.g., risky investments) or if the driver is reckless (e.g., no process to monitor speed), you can get injured or killed (worry about running out of money, or worse yet, actually run out of money!).

The WorryFree Retirement Process allows the consumer to decide what type of vehicle they wish to drive, based on their unique circumstances, their tastes and their destination. The Retirement Specialist's job is to give them what they want. This process differs from traditional financial planning – my training years ago. Traditional planning (products) is based on needs and assumptions, not wants and realities. But a *process*, is ongoing and ever-changing. A traditional financial plan, on the other hand, is based on the financial assumptions created by the customer. The planner just fills in the blanks. The traditional financial plan is usually doomed for failure because at some point the assumptions will need to be modified. Assumptions are merely predictions of the future. You remember what happens when you "assume," don't you?

Let's have some fun by listening in on a typical interview between a today's "traditional" financial planner and a prospective client:

> Planner *(with a happy face): Thanks for filling out this [twenty page] questionnaire and getting all of these financial documents together for me.*

Step Eight: Have Fun

Consumer *(with a happy face)*: *You're welcome. (Face grimaces somewhat.) It took more time than I thought.*

Planner *(with a more let's get down to business face): Now, before I come up with a financial plan, we need to make some assumptions.*

Consumer *(funny look on his/her face): What kind of assumptions?*

Planner *(gets excited knowing he/she gets to talk about all the great products his company offers): Oh, things like: how much money you think you'll need for retirement; what rate of return we should assume on your investments; how much life insurance you need; how much you'll need to send the kids to college; stuff like that...*

Consumer *(with a confused and troubled look on his/her face): Oh...well, I don't really know the answers* *to all of that, that's why I came to you.*

Planner *(seeing once again, that here sits another consumer who doesn't know anything about predicting the future): Oh, we've got lots of experts here at XYZ company who will help us with that...don't you worry. (Planner puts on his more serious face to get client focused again on products.) So, let's start with rate of return...what should we assume you'll make on your 401(k) between now and retirement?*

Consumer *(puzzled look on his face): I don't know, what do your people say I should expect to make?*

Planner *(quickly reaches for a slick four-color chart showing an arrow going straight up): Well, as you can see here, over the past 50 years, our funds have averaged 75%, so just to be conservative, I think you should assume 12%.*

Step Eight: Have Fun

Consumer *(with troubled look on his/her face): Well, let's see, my 401(k) did real well in the 90s but it's down almost 50% since 9-11... So, how do I figure that out?*

Planner *(shrugging shoulders): Good point. Let's be "real" conservative and use 10%!*

You laugh, but this is what I see on a regular basis. Prospective clients contact me wanting my opinion about their finances. In many cases, they are worried because no one is helping them understand how to safely manage their financial affairs in a simple and easy to understand manner. The majority of folks I meet are simply hard working folks, frustrated over assumptions that didn't quite pan out as expected. That's because you can't predict (assume) the future and neither can the "experts." Will Rogers was reputed to have said, "Always think the worst, and you'll never be disappointed." Now, while I don't totally agree with this, I do when it comes to making "assumptions" about the future. In my practice, I never assume more than 5% on growth of assets. That's because – over the long term – 5%

isn't as easy to get as you might think. Sometimes, I'll even use 3% just for the "fun" of it. When you factor in taxes, inflation, fees, insurance premiums and much more, one might argue that even 3% is on the high side.

The traditional financial planning path can sometimes lead to nowhere. There is no path to follow, no way to truly monitor your progress, because traditional advice is based on needs rather than wants and dreams. Needs constantly change, but a clear vision of the future (wants, hopes and dreams) doesn't.

The WorryFree Retirement Process is unique in that it starts with a powerful conversation about you. The conversation is centered on your vision of the ideal retirement. It's based on who you are and what you want. It explores all of your fears and worries. The Process identifies those things in the world that you can control and those you can't. It allows you to focus on what matters, so you can establish a safe way to get there. It's a conversation that includes products, but is not dominated by them. The products ("The where") pale in comparison to the Process ("The how to get there"). Listening to people's dreams isn't easy. It takes one who is passionate about the truth. One who truly enjoys helping people reach their full potential. The vast majority of financial advisors I meet (and I've met hundreds over the years) are trained in financial products and how to sell them. Their training comes from either needs-based institutions of learning, or the financial institutions themselves (those who manufacture the financial products). Helping people create a WorryFree Retirement goes beyond the "products" of financial planning. And as I see it, there are very few financial advisors who are equipped and willing to take the time to help others Perfect Their Walk in retirement.

So how do you know if you can trust a financial advisor? How do you know that he or she is more in this game for them, rather than you? Ask them! Why not? They get to ask you all those nosey questions about your personal finances, so why not get nosey with them? Talkin' about having fun...here are a few "fun" questions I recommend you ask when speaking with any financial advisor or "expert" on money:

- *How did you get into this business?*

- *Why did you get into this business?*

- *How long have you been advising people about money?*

- *Where do you get your information? Who or what is your biggest source of information?*

- *Do you work for any financial institution or simply work with them?*

- *Are you required to sell so much of any one product to keep your job? Does anyone tell you what has to be sold to your customers, or do you have the authority to decide?*

- *Tell me about your wife and kids. If not applicable, tell me about your folks. Where did you grow up? What formal education do you have?*

Step Eight: Have Fun

- *If I disagree with you on any recommendations you make, are you going to get mad and look at me like I'm a complete idiot?*

Remember, it's *your* money, not theirs. They should be "applying" for the job of helping you reach your goals in life. It should be considered a privilege for any advisor to work for people who are nice to work for, and fun to be around – people like you, right? Incidentally, I don't do well with overly serious people. Don't get me wrong. I take their lives seriously, and I consider their money a serious topic. But if they won't work on having some fun, they usually move on to someone else. Life's too short to not have fun. Let's face it, none of us is getting out of this deal alive anyway, and you sure can't take it with you. So, as my mother-in-law always says: "Let's have some fun!"

Step Eight: Have Fun
(Just Be Sure To Bring Someone With You)

THE WORRYFREE RETIREMENT™ GUIDE: TWO-MINUTE WALK

If you're not having fun at what you're doing, it may not be worth doing at all. I define fun as something that brings joy and contentment. It's a sense of accomplishment in what you're doing on a daily basis. It's what your walk should be about. But there's a problem: people, places, things and circumstances will try to rob your joy. These "joy robbers" will attempt to steer you off the walking path. In order to keep the joy-robbers at bay, I've created a quick exercise called the Personal Fun Protector™. It's a gauge to see what's robbing your joy and how to get it back.

Step 8 Have Fun (Just Be Sure To Bring Someone With You)

I'M WORRIED...	Not Worried	Somewhat Worried	Very Worried
that I'm not having fun at work anymore.	1 2 3	4 5 6 7	8 9 10
that I don't have any friends to enjoy life with.	1 2 3	4 5 6 7	8 9 10
that the people I'm hanging with are robbing my joy.	1 2 3	4 5 6 7	8 9 10
that I'm wasting time on things like TV, the internet, etc.	1 2 3	4 5 6 7	8 9 10
that being disorganized is costing me time and money.	1 2 3	4 5 6 7	8 9 10
that I'm spending too much time on the road/commuting to work.	1 2 3	4 5 6 7	8 9 10
that I don't get along with family members.	1 2 3	4 5 6 7	8 9 10
that I'm not involved in activities with my family.	1 2 3	4 5 6 7	8 9 10
that I'm afraid to spend and have fun with my money.	1 2 3	4 5 6 7	8 9 10
that I'm spending too much money on myself, and not others.	1 2 3	4 5 6 7	8 9 10

MY BIGGEST WORRY IS...

_____

_____

(transfer to ActionPlanner on page 177)

Step Nine

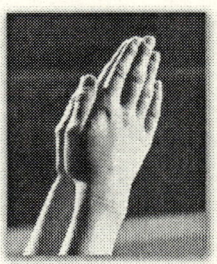

Be Thankful

"What in the world do we have to be thankful for? Everything!" ~ Tony Walker

One of the best ways to attack worry is to be thankful. When hard work doesn't cut it, when you don't feel like having fun, thinking "thankful" thoughts may just be the best medicine for worry.

In my own life, I notice that when I'm thankful, I'm humble. And when I feel humble, I don't worry. A thankful heart is one that doesn't get caught up in what you don't have (for example, wishing you had your neighbor's house), but takes stock in what you do have (a nice home that's plenty big, thank you very much). When I worry, or see others worry,

Step Nine: Be Thankful

I see a sign of an ungrateful heart. Worry tells me when I'm forgetting to be thankful.

Maybe it's just an age thing or something, but when I pick up our local newspaper, the first place I turn to is the obituary column. I even find myself – in the secrecy of my car – tuning in to the obituary report broadcast daily on the local radio station. I see people my age, dying! As I write this book, I was just informed that one of my teammates from our high school basketball team was murdered just this week. Whenever I feel ungrateful, or really worried, I think of death. The sting of death will stop anyone, even the biggest, most famous of them all. When you and I die, there's no do-over. You can't take a mulligan (that's a golf term for getting to take a free swing at the ball – for those who don't know). There's no more fun, no more family, and no more time. As my son Anthony likes to say... It's over!

So the next time you're having a pity party and feeling ungrateful for what you have, think about the alternative. Think about today. Because today really is all you've got. Be thankful.

At the time I began this book, an unprecedented tsunami hit parts of Asia, the result of an earthquake in the Indian Ocean. The tsunami devastated the shores of Indonesia, Sri Lanka, Thailand, south India and other countries. Before that happened, I had no idea what a tsunami was. Maybe you were similarly ignorant. Well, after all of the news coverage I think most of us have a much clearer notion of what a tsunami is, but in case you don't, just think of a huge tidal wave that comes out of nowhere and sweeps over the land with a force great enough to kill hundreds of thousands of people in a single bound. The tsunami that recently hit Asia took the lives of over 150,000 people. Like most tragedies, this one hit when people least expected it. Much of the news footage shows a beautiful coastline with people having fun. Then, out of nowhere, the ocean recedes away from the coast line. You can see the people look on in wonder (just like I would have done). This strange, peaceful sight was beautiful, something no one had ever seen. But in just an instant, the waters that had once receded came back into the shoreline with a vengeance. People watched helplessly as giant waves overtook them. Most died. In an instant, their lives were finished.

Step Nine: Be Thankful

Are you thankful yet?

As I was putting the finishing touches on the manuscript for this book, Hurricane Katrina, a Category 5 storm, hit the Gulf Coast of the United States, all but destroying New Orleans and several cities in Mississippi and Alabama. People had a little more time to prepare for this than they had for the tsunami, but many of the poorest, sickest and most helpless citizens were unable to escape the ravages of the storm. The evacuation plans, such as they were, did not take into account the thousands of people who did not have their own transportation. These people couldn't just pack the kids and the dog and their most treasured gadgets and gizmos into their SUV, put $100 worth of gas in the tank, and drive down Interstate 10 to check into a comfy hotel to wait out the storm. Even those who did manage to escape via buses and other public transportation were faced with the prospect of being herded into temporary shelters, knowing they had no home to return to. And by the time Katrina was finished, some of America's most beautiful cities looked a lot like the coast of India or Thailand after that tsunami.

Are you feeling thankful yet?

Did you know that many people around the world work for wages of $3.00 a day? I didn't say $3.00 per hour; I said $3.00 per day! And we thought our country's minimum wage of $5.75 an hour was chump change. Americans should be the most thankful people the world has ever known. But we're not. I realize there is poverty in America, and that even without all the "gadgets and gizmos" I've talked about, it is enormously challenging to live a decent middle-class life in the US making minimum wage. I am not unsympathetic to the plight of the poor and the "working poor." I also realize that after Hurricane Katrina hit, many Americans were left without homes and jobs. Compared to the rest of the world, however, Americans have more money than they know what to do with. If you are a member of Middle America, and all of your basic needs are being met, you should feel blessed. And if you feel like you don't have any money, maybe you need to take a trip to the recently ravaged shorelines of India or Thailand. (Or, closer to home – to New Orleans or Biloxi, Mississippi.) That'll wake you up. We look at our 10-year-old car as a jalopy; in parts of the world (and even some

Step Nine: Be Thankful

neighborhoods in the US), it's considered a limousine. We drop our old clothes off at Goodwill; people in some parts of the world would love the opportunity to shop at Goodwill. Is it any wonder that the world sees us as materialistic. Maybe they're right! Or, maybe it's because we just don't seem very thankful for what we have.

I'm concerned that Americans are ill prepared for what could possibly be a huge financial tsunami (or hurricane, if you prefer). Our spending habits are riding as high as the economy. We see, we want, we buy (or borrow). Granddad never bought so much because he never wanted so much. He was thankful to have what he had and enjoy it for as long as possible. My granddad was thankful for what he had because that's all he could get.

Today's consumer mentality is like the tourist in Indonesia or Thailand sitting on the beach before the tsunami. Everything is good. The world is so peaceful and enjoyable. And then, in one fell swoop, the waters recede, and a horrendous wave of tragedy sweeps our dreams right off the beach. The thought of such a financial tsunami is real. America is not immune. Just look at the financial fallout from 9/11.

Perfecting Your Walk includes a daily dose of thanksgiving. And to be thankful, you've got to be humble. You have to be humbled by the fact that nothing stays the same, and what you have today, could be swept away tomorrow. Remember what I said earlier about the importance of contentment? A thankful heart is a content heart.

Prospective clients often ask me how they are doing financially as compared to everyone else their age. It's a good question, and a natural one to ask, but it's totally irrelevant. In the words of my late father, "Who cares!" Why base your financial attitude on someone else's financial altitude? Remember, it's difficult to size up someone's life by sitting at a ball game with them, watching your kids play, or talking with them at a neighborhood cookout. You are seeing what they want you to see. And one of the things they no doubt want you to see is that they aren't worried about their money and their retirement. I, on the other hand, get a bird's eye view of the total picture. I can look at your neighbors with their big house, three cars, and boat, and see their WorryMeter. I understand what fears and concerns they have. And I know when someone is thankful and content, or running scared.

Many people coming to me for financial advice have loads of money. These are good people who have their own concerns in life. I know that what is most important in my life may not be most important to them. What makes me thankful may not make them thankful. The challenge I face is to do my best to create a WorryFree Retirement™ based on their goals and visions for the future. Clarifying their vision is such an important first step in the process.

Remember, a destination that has a clear path, and goals and habits to help you stay on that path, will keep you focused on your daily walk. Your future walk is laid out, so you'll be less distracted by all of the influences that tell you that you should have more. If you have clarity about your future, be thankful for it. If you don't have that clarity yet, be thankful that you still have time to achieve it.

At this point, you may be saying, "Tony, it's not that simple. You don't know my entire situation. I just lost my job and I came home to discover that my wife of 30 years ran off with the milkman. I had to file bankruptcy last week. What in the world do I have to be thankful for?"

I'll say it again: "Just be thankful. Thankful you're alive and can do something about your walk. Be thankful for the opportunities that the world has to offer you. Whatever you're going through today, deal with it. Take action by being thankful. As long as you're a living, breathing human being, be thankful!"

The WorryFree Retirement Process requires a new mind-set. It requires us to be thankful and content with what we have. Of course, this does not rule out improving our situation or even trying to accumulate "more" to fill real needs or wants. What is required is a core of contentment that is unaffected by having "more" or "less." The WorryFree Retirement Process provides tools so we can monitor our progress along the life's journey. It reminds us to be thankful for today, since we can't control tomorrow. We begin to not only accept change, but to look

Step Nine: Be Thankful

forward to it. Being thankful will provide protection when this country (and your wallet) encounter another financial tsunami. Thankfulness might not cure all of your worries, but it sure will treat the symptoms.

Step Nine: Be Thankful

THE WORRYFREE RETIREMENT™ GUIDE: TWO-MINUTE WALK

This next two-minute walk will help you inventory the things you are most thankful for. The key to overcoming the bad times is to look at the good times. Thankfulness is a skill that must be developed. It's almost like learning art. You must build thanksgiving habits into your daily walk. It won't be easy. We live in a society that doesn't value thankfulness and humility. You will need a guide to help you stay focused on your ultimate destination. Thankfulness is a choice. This exercise will help you gain focus so you can include being thankful in your walk.

Step 9 Be Thankful

I'M WORRIED...	Not Worried	Somewhat Worried	Very Worried
that I'm not thankful for my spouse.	1 2 3	4 5 6 7	8 9 10
that I'm not thankful for my kids (family).	1 2 3	4 5 6 7	8 9 10
that I'm not thankful for my job or special interest.	1 2 3	4 5 6 7	8 9 10
that I'm not thankful for my health.	1 2 3	4 5 6 7	8 9 10
that I'm not thankful for my income and/or finances.	1 2 3	4 5 6 7	8 9 10
that I'm not thankful for the community in which I live.	1 2 3	4 5 6 7	8 9 10
that I'm not thankful for my gifts and talents.	1 2 3	4 5 6 7	8 9 10
that I'm not thankful for the country in which I live.	1 2 3	4 5 6 7	8 9 10
that I'm not thankful for my heritage and background.	1 2 3	4 5 6 7	8 9 10
that I'm not thankful for faith in God.	1 2 3	4 5 6 7	8 9 10

MY BIGGEST WORRY IS...

_____

_____

(transfer to ActionPlanner on page 177)

Step Ten

Trust God With The Rest

"Trust in God creates confidence in the future."
~ Tony Walker

Depending on your favorite poll, between 80 to 90 percent of Americans "say" they believe in God. What about you? Do you believe in God? If so, do you trust in Him; particularly when it comes to your retirement?

Here's what I find interesting about all of these polls...with so many of us saying we believe in God, why are we still so worried about the future? With the wealth and prosperity this country has to offer, how in the world could anyone be worried?

Step Ten: Trust God With The Rest

I interview worried people everyday. I receive emails and phone calls from people watching my television show who admit to worrying about their money. Being human, no matter how good things appear to be, we still find reason to worry. We worry our money won't last through retirement. We worry about our children as we watch them struggle financially. One would think with so many of us "believing" in God, that we would put our worries aside and just "trust" Him. Folks I meet tell me they believe in God, but they don't trust Him. How can I prove this? By their level of worry.

Several years ago, my wife and I took a trip to Arizona. While there, we drove up to "see" the Grand Canyon. Anxious to view the world's biggest hole in the ground, we entered Grand Canyon National Park and quickly pulled over at the first view area. We stepped out of the car, and together, "saw" the majesty and wonder of THE Grand Canyon! Granted, while Susan and I didn't actually watch God create the "eighth wonder of the world," we trusted that He was the only one with the ability to pull it off. For us, "seeing" the Grand Canyon was confirmation that God, not man, had to have created such an awesome sight.

While we can all agree that man is talented, he's not that talented. Case in point: just look at the circumstances surrounding the recent flooding of New Orleans as a result of Hurricane Katrina. We'll compare man's talents against that of nature – God.

How did the city of New Orleans come to be? Apparently, years ago, some venture capitalists "saw" the potential for big bucks by developing land along the Gulf of Mexico. While most of the land along the gulf coast is at sea level, New Orleans is not… it's "below" sea level! I don't know much about sea level, but it would seem obvious that if you're going to construct a city below water, you better figure out a way to stay dry. But these were not your ordinary venture capitalists.

Not to be discouraged by a little water, someone comes up with the notion of constructing a concrete levee to "hold back" the ocean so the city won't flood (sounds like the same guy who thought up Social Security). So, with the opportunity of making boat loads of money, they design and build levees to keep the folks of New Orleans separated from the ocean. For many years, the levees hold. New Orleans grows and prospers.

The people rejoice and celebrate by standing on balconies, throwing colorful beads at would-be tourists.

Despite repeated warnings that the levee may not withstand hurricane like conditions, the residents and politicians of New Orleans continue their prosperous journey.

Important Rule: When building a levee, remember "God's" Golden rule: It might hold for a little while, but sooner or later the forces of nature will bring it down. (*Moral to the Rule: because we're human, it's much easier to trust in the ingenuity of man – a concrete levee – rather than the power of God's creation – a powerful body of water with the unpredictable nature of a hurricane*).

We construct our own levees all the time; they just happen to be "financial" levees. They come in all shapes and sizes: sure-fire financial products, strategies and other magic bullets promising to hold back the tides of uncertainty. Sadly, just like the levees constructed in New Orleans, most of these man-made products can't withstand the hurricanes (inflation, taxes, market risk, death). That's because a WorryFree Retirement cannot be based on products alone. Financial products must be part of a well managed process; a process which includes your hopes, dreams and concerns.

Understanding the desire to control our own destiny, God equips us to take charge by working hard and being responsible. He never intends for us to be in control - that's His job. That's good, because being in charge means someone else with more authority – like God – is ultimately responsible for the outcome. And that takes the burden and worry off us.

So how do you trust God with the rest? In my own personal life, I've discovered that the only true source of accurate information on this matter of trust is the Bible. Contained in the world's best selling book is all that a person ever needs to know about worry (lack of trust) and how to overcome it (by faith).

At the age of 30 (I'm now 45), I didn't know much about trusting God with the rest. Heck, I didn't even own a Bible. The Bible seemed intimidating; an impractical volume of fancy English

Step Ten: Trust God With The Rest

terminology complete with hundreds of difficult names and stories to keep up with. Not knowing where to begin, someone suggested the book of Psalms. To me, the book of Psalms is where the soul finds expression. I began reading about a man by the name of David. David, who started his career as a young lad herding sheep, became King (what a vision) to an entire group of people. As King, David enjoyed unlimited authority. People were under his control. They placed their trust in him because "he was the law." Yet, with all of David's man-made authority, David slips. His levy (power and authority) crashes. The flood of New Orleans is nothing compared to the mess this man created. So what does David do? What any good politician does in times of crisis: blame somebody else. Cover up the worry by trying to put a band-aid on the problem. Since David was in charge, why not try "fixing" his worries? Trusting in his own abilities, David plunges deeper into the murky waters of his personal hurricane. Finally, after much trial and tribulation, David remembers his past; a time in his life in which he placed his trust in God, instead of position. Eventually, David's journey leads him to conclude the following "The Lord will 'perfect' that which worries me."

Here's the point: God didn't create us to worry about the things of the world. But since we're human, and live in the real world, he knew we would. When we worry, we're basically telling God, "I know you promised to provide me food, clothing and shelter, but how come I don't have as much stuff as the guy down the street?"

The way I "see" it, if God has control over the Grand Canyon, hurricanes and wayward Kings, surely he can help us worry less about our money. The secret ingredient is trust. Placing your trust in Him puts you on a path for Perfecting Your Walk. With scripture as your guide, your walk will begin to resemble the voice of wisdom and reason, rather than resemble a life of fits and starts. The Bible is quite simple and easy to understand, when read with a desire to trust in the author. Read about the life of David (I Samuel). "See" how God 'perfected' him by replacing his worries with trust.

How about you? What keeps you up at night worrying? Is your vision of a WorryFree Retirement assembled on the shifting sand of man's financial levees, or is it built upon the solid rock of God's promises? Who do you trust? And more importantly, "what" do you trust in. Do you believe what you know and know what you believe?

Perfecting Your Walk is not easy. It is not something you do overnight. It is a lifetime process. It's about a journey that's bigger than you and me. Our 'perfecting' is focusing on doing the very best we can, to be who we are meant to be, and doing the things we are meant to do. Perfecting our walk isn't an easy process. It is extremely difficult and challenging, but the rewards are tremendous.

"Trusting God with the rest" is a part of this process. It acknowledges our responsibility for our actions and accomplishments in life. Deep down inside, we all know our short comings and flaws. We realize that there is a creator who made us the way we are - warts and all! We can truly trust Him to guide us and protect us on our journey. Our responsibility is to trust and obey. We really aren't on this journey alone. His message is clear and undeniable.

So what does the Bible have to say about retirement?

Nothing!

While there's a multitude of pages dedicated to working hard, having fun and being thankful, little is said of quitting work and playing golf for the rest of your life. As I have noted earlier, work is an important part of who we are, particularly in America. Consider what you tell people when you are meeting them for the first time. Usually, the first words out of your mouth have something to do with what you do for a living. In some cultures it is considered impolite to ask someone what kind of work they do. In others, it is simply not considered important enough to talk about. Not so in our society. That's because we all believe that work is part of our walk.

When I wrote about mission statements, I noted that work should give us purpose and great meaning. This is not just for the sake of personal fulfillment; there is more to it than that. Work honors God because we are using His gifts, our hands and minds to accomplish His good purpose. Work is also therapeutic. It

Step Ten: Trust God With The Rest

takes our minds off the world. Work helps us focus our efforts on God. We work so that others may be provided for. Not only does work help us provide for our families, but for those less fortunate – widows, orphans and the poor.

Of course, there's nothing wrong in God's economy with planning for the future. Just like Granddad did, saving and investing wisely, having fun and enjoying the fruits of our labor is quite alright. (I think God would even enjoy watching *Johnny Carson*.) However, God never intended for us to be consumed with making huge amounts of money so we could build bigger barns to store it in. Trusting God is the most important element to Perfecting Your Walk – and trusting in God is not about money!

There's nothing wrong with hard work, but I honestly don't believe God wants to see Granddad – or you – working 80 hours a week. Physically, Granddad can't work as hard as he once did, and maybe you can't either. Folks wear down over time. Your weight shifts and so does your level of energy. That doesn't mean you can't continue to be productive. In fact, some of the most "WorryFree" folks I meet are those in the 70-plus age group who are both physically and mentally active in the workplace. Remember that 79-year-old, peanut butter and jelly eating doctor I mentioned in a previous chapter? When older folks work, their minds work too. That's just how God wired us. Putting Adam and Even to work may have been a "punishment" at the very beginning, but it was also a gift and a blessing. Through work, we may not be able to recreate the Garden of Eden, but we can certainly make the world better for ourselves and others.

Chapters one through nine reflect my findings in working closely with people over the past 20 years. The concept of creating a WorryFree Retirement is based on my belief that we all want that. All of us have different wants, but as humans, we all desire to be happy and content. As we have observed, however, the world has another take on life. The world says that what we have, no matter how much or how little, isn't enough. The world tells us that happiness can only be found through *doing* (making something out of ourselves and our money). God, on the other hand, says peace and contentment are found in *being* (placing our trust in Him). The world says you win the game by scoring more points than your opponent; God says you win the game by staying the course.

My mission in life is to help people worry less about their money. That's because I have come to understand that you can't trust in money. A financial Tsunami can strike at any time. There really are no guarantees when it comes to retirement. ✳ The purpose of The WorryFree Retirement Process is to give you tools to help you worry less about your money so you can further your personal partnership with God.

By now, you should have a clearer vision of your "perfect" retirement. It should be one which embraces a desire to become WorryFree. My hope is that your vision for retirement is much different than when we first started. It is also my hope that your course in life will change as a result of our walk together thus far. You should be encouraged knowing that your journey in life is not about money, but simply living life to the best of your ability. The "perfect" retirement on earth doesn't exist. No matter how hard you try, you will still encounter worry. But it will not define you. It won't keep you up nights, or have you pacing the floor during the day. Instead, when you do encounter worry you will be able to accept it as the gift it is; yet another reminder that you need God, and that God is in control.

So if you are burdened about your money, your future or your past, if retirement is something that scares you to death, just stop worrying! Put your trust in God and begin to review the steps throughout this book. These ten steps will help you build upon this trust. I have also listed a few Bible passages that deal with each step. If you don't have a Bible, go buy one. There's even a "Bible For Dummies" in print. One really does exist! Read it with the same enthusiasm and anticipation one might expect from reading a great novel. Trust me, it's even better than "seeing" the Grand Canyon. Even though the Bible does not specifically address the concept of retirement as we know it, God will speak to you about retirement – and every other aspect of your life – in ways you may have never considered.

Step Ten: Trust God With The Rest

THE WORRYFREE RETIREMENT™ GUIDE: TWO-MINUTE WALK

I've certainly enjoyed serving as your guide; however, for our last walk together, I'll defer that task to God. That's because I'm human, just like you. So let's turn to God's Word, the Bible, for help. The Bible is our road map. It will help us understand more about our money, possessions and, yes, our retirement. Trust in His word serves as a light on a darkened path. The Word of God makes the crooked path straight. Like the Psalmist David, may we trust in God to perfect that which worries us. Here's the ultimate road map for Perfecting Our Walk in retirement. May God bless you in your journey!

Step 10 Trust God With the Rest

I'M WORRIED...	Not Worried	Somewhat Worried	Very Worried
that my current retirement vision is becoming confusing.	1 2 3	4 5 6 7	8 9 10
that my lack of a clear vision is keeping me frustrated.	1 2 3	4 5 6 7	8 9 10
that I'm stuck in the past and can't enjoy the present.	1 2 3	4 5 6 7	8 9 10
that my lack of financial wisdom is affecting my walk.	1 2 3	4 5 6 7	8 9 10
that I can't seem to deal with my human flaws – warts and all.	1 2 3	4 5 6 7	8 9 10
that God is displeased with the path I'm on.	1 2 3	4 5 6 7	8 9 10
that I'm not working hard enough for my family.	1 2 3	4 5 6 7	8 9 10
that I don't enjoy life as I should.	1 2 3	4 5 6 7	8 9 10
That I'm taking things for granted.	1 2 3	4 5 6 7	8 9 10
that I have trouble trusting God with the rest.	1 2 3	4 5 6 7	8 9 10

MY BIGGEST WORRY IS...

_____

_____

(transfer to ActionPlanner on page 177)

Scripture Reference

STEP 1: *Determine Your Level Of Worry –*
Matthew 6:31; Philippians 4:6

STEP 2: *Create Your Own Retirement Vision –*
Jeremiah 29:11; Proverbs 3:6

STEP 3: *Say Goodbye To Granddad's Retirement –*
Ecclesiastes 1:4; Proverbs 16:3

STEP 4: *Know The Rules Of The Game –*
Psalm 73:24

STEP 5: *Admit You're Human –*
Psalm 39:4; Romans 7:19

STEP 6: *Taking Responsibility –*
Proverbs 9:9; 1 Corinthians 3:8

STEP 7: *Work Hard (But Slow Down) –*
Ecclesiastes 2:24; Proverbs 10: 4, 13:11

STEP 8: *Have Fun (Just Be Sure To Bring Someone With You) –*
1 Timothy 6:17; Ecclesiastes 3:13; Philippians 4:4

STEP 9: *Be Thankful –*
1 Thessalonians 1:2; 2 Corinthians 9:8

STEP 10: *Trust God With The Rest –*
Matthew 6:34; Psalms 37:5; 40:4; 62:8;
Proverbs 16:20; 1 Timothy 6:17

The WorryFree Retirement™
Commitment

It has been said that the journey of a thousand miles begins with the first step. Your walk through retirement – and for the rest of your life – is no different. Remember, a vision without action is but a daydream. And the first place to start is by simply committing your thoughts on paper and finding a trusted friend who will serve as your walking partner.

I, _____(your name) agree to take action on my biggest worry, as outlined in the WorryFree Retirement Action Planner. I will do so with the intention of reducing, or eliminating, this worry altogether. I wish to do this so that I may enjoy life more and worry less about my future. My walking partner will be _____ (their name). I will commit to reviewing this plan with my walking partner no later than _____ (write in a date no later than one week from today).

        Signed: _____

        Today's date: _____

I _____(name of walking partner) do hereby agree to assume the role as your walking partner. By signing below, I acknowledge that I have reviewed your Action Plan and will help you monitor your progress as needed.

        Signed: _____

        Today's date: _____

Assuming you have completed the first step toward Perfecting Your Walk -- finding a walking partner and completing the Commitment Letter -- let's begin that all important second step of reviewing your ActionPlanner, located on the following pages.

Upon completion of The ActionPlanner, you will be in a better position to focus your efforts on reducing -or even eliminating -your biggest worry. If, at this stage of your walk, you aren't comfortable dealing with "your biggest" worry, select one you feel you can tackle right away. The key is to keep walking...even if you're taking baby steps for now.

And finally, after completing The ActionPlanner, answer the thought-provoking questions listed on page 178. These questions are designed to help you clarify your thinking by taking responsibility so you won't have to procrastinate any longer.

Good luck!

The WorryFree Retirement™
ActionPlanner

Page	Two-Minute Walk Chapter Exercises
15	**Step One:** *Determine Your Level of Worry*
27	**Step Two:** *Create Your Own Retirement Vision*
43	**Step Three:** *Say Goodbye to Granddad's Retirement*
59	**Step Four:** *Know The Rules of The Game*
82	**Step Five:** *Admit You're Human*
104	**Step Six:** *Take Responsibility*
122	**Step Seven:** *Work Hard (Just Slow Down)*
145	**Step Eight:** *Have Fun (Just Be Sure To Bring Someone With You)*
157	**Step Nine:** *Be Thankful*
172	**Step Ten:** *Trust God With The Rest*

My Biggest Worry is...*(list below)*	Level of Worry (1-10)
(add up all responses) Your Score	

(see reverse side)

Of the ten worries listed on your Personal ActionPlanner, which "one" worries you the most?
_____
_____

When did you begin worrying about it?
_____
_____

Why do you think you're so worried about it?
_____
_____

Who, besides yourself, might be affected by this worry?
_____
_____

Where - or who - could you go to for help?
_____
_____

How would you feel if you could eliminate this worry?
_____
_____

What will happen if you don't deal with this worry?
_____
_____

What one action would you be willing to take "today" to reduce this worry?
_____
_____

"The path that lies ahead doesn't have to be one of worry......

...follow your vision and take time to enjoy the journey."

~ Tony

About the Book

Retirement…whose idea was this anyway! And where in the world are you going with it?

Today, millions of hard-working Americans frantically search for that dream retirement like Granddad once enjoyed. You know how it's supposed to go; land a secure job with a big company, work hard for thirty or forty years, then, on that magic day, you retire with a guaranteed pension income and plenty of "mailbox money," compliments of Social Security. If your retirement dream looks like this, wake up!

In case you haven't noticed, things have changed a lot since Granddads' day. Today's consumer is overspent and "under-saved." Worried their money won't last through retirement, Middle Americans feel hopelessly lost. Impersonal financial institutions, 1-800 numbers, inattentive financial advisors, hundreds of financial magazines, and newsletters - even the occasional hyper-active financial talk show host - simply adds more worry to their retirement.

In Perfecting Your Walk in Retirement: 10 Steps to a WorryFree Retirement, Tony Walker brings over twenty years of level-headed experience and thinking to a financial world that's short on both. Armed with his unique blend of humor, financial counseling experience and sound money principals, Tony will help you create your own vision for retirement, a vision based on what you want, not what someone else says you should expect.

Regardless of whether you're retired, retiring soon, or just beginning to think about it, this book will give you the tools necessary to craft a realistic game plan so you and your family can begin…

For more information about the WorryFree Retirment Process, go to
www.WorryFreeFinancial.com

About the Author

A native and resident of the Bluegrass state of Kentucky, Tony Walker began his financial career in 1984, working with his father-in-law in a small insurance firm in Bowling Green, Kentucky. After just a few months of helping people protect their property, Tony realized that most people didn't have a plan for protecting their future.

In addition to his formal education in psychology and communications, Tony holds several advanced financial planning degrees. He continues to research and gain new knowledge regarding all aspects of retirement planning. Tony is committed to giving people a liberating WorryFree perspective about life and money.

As host of the long-standing TV show, Your Money Matters, Tony has developed a reputation for his ability to clearly and concisely communicate complex financial solutions for the average person.

Tony is married to his high school sweetheart, Susan. They have three children, Phillip, Lacey and Anthony, and two lovable miniature dachshunds, Holly and Hershey "The Wonder Dog".

Printed in the United States
42012LVS00007B/157-255